"In *Welcome to Adulting*, Jonatha[n] trivial and more time on the transf[o]... gives advice on how to live an adul[t]... love it! JP's not worried about the adult ways of this world but rather the adult matters that are out of this world. Enjoy the ride."

Kyle Idleman, pastor and author of *Not a Fan*
and *Grace Is Greater*

"Jonathan so candidly and beautifully breaks down the myths of life after college and leaves us with a roadmap we'll return to again and again, no matter how old we are."

Jennie Allen, author of *Nothing to Prove*; founder and visionary
of the IF:Gathering

"I try to only listen to voices that are living what they are saying. JP is one of those. This book isn't just an amazing book but also one that has been fought for and lived out and extracted from years of pursuing Jesus and helping others. I hope it blesses you as much as it did me!"

Jefferson Bethke, *New York Times* bestselling author
of *Jesus > Religion*

"In the midst of confusion and half-truths, *Welcome to Adulting* is a Scripture-soaked survival guide. Read this book and drop your anchor in the blood-bought truth of Jesus."

Nick Hall, founder and chief communicator for PULSE; author of
RESET: Jesus Changes Everything

"There aren't many leaders in America who have the experience working with the next generation like Jonathan Pokluda. I'm so grateful he's put pen to paper on helping shape the future for so many who need a guide! Don't miss this book!"

Clay Scroggins, lead pastor of North Point Community Church

"There is a reason that thousands of young professionals listen when Jonathan Pokluda speaks. He is a worthy guide for all who are navigating the tempestuous seas of young adulthood. I am grateful he has given this book as a gift to the world."

Ben Stuart, pastor of Passion City Church, DC,
and author of *Single, Dating, Engaged, Married*

"*Welcome to Adulting* is filled with personal stories and timeless truths all told in a winsome and memorable way that makes every minute spent reading one of the wisest investments a person could make. This is not just a book for the next generation of leaders to read but one that people serious about forming the next generation of leaders should memorize."

Todd Wagner, senior pastor of Watermark Community Church;
author of *Come and See*

"I have watched JP fight for these chapters over the last decade! Mostly in the pages of his own life. My prayer is that God would use them to bring healing and freedom in your life as he has in mine."

Shane Barnard, Shane and Shane Music

"As a new Christian recently graduated from college, I found myself unprepared to deal with many of the monumental, life-altering decisions staring me in the face. In *Welcome to Adulting*, my good friend JP speaks truth into these challenges in a way that will make an adult life an abundant life."

Brandon Slay, Olympic wrestling champion and executive director of the Pennsylvania RTC

"One day with Jonathan Pokluda and you will be changed forever. His love for Christ is undeniable, and he shares it with every person he comes in contact with. This boldness he displays daily is something all believers should experience, and this book captures that so well."

Chad Hedrick, Olympic gold medalist and world champion

"JP speaks with clarity, candor, and conviction. You can't help but sense that he has tasted and is daily seeking to feast on the freedom and fullness found in wholehearted pursuit of Jesus Christ. *Welcome to Adulting* is a unique, refreshing, and invaluable compass to anyone navigating the new waters of adulthood."

Timothy Ateek, executive director of Breakaway Ministries

"Honest. Sincere. Real. This is who JP is and this is how he communicates. Combining personal experiences with wisdom from Scripture, this book will serve as a pathway to spiritual maturity. I highly recommend it for anyone serious about their spiritual growth."

Jarrett Stephens, teaching pastor of Prestonwood Baptist Church and author of *The Mountains Are Calling*

"Jonathan writes from a place of passion for those moving into adulthood here and now. His insights are accessible and simple, and I would recommend this book to all parents and leaders who are tasked with bringing a new generation into adulthood."

Casey Tygrett, author of *Becoming Curious: A Spiritual Practice of Asking Questions*

"I'm constantly amazed with how JP can tactfully show my generation how the 'good news' we're so desperately chasing is utterly minuscule compared to *the* Good News. *Welcome to Adulting* is a guide that comes from a posture of vulnerable experience and biblical reassurance that God's way is *better*."

Grant Skeldon, founder of Initiative Network

*welcome to ADULTING

NAVIGATING FAITH, FRIENDSHIP, FINANCES, AND THE FUTURE

JONATHAN "JP" POKLUDA
WITH KEVIN McCONAGHY

BakerBooks

a division of Baker Publishing Group
Grand Rapids, Michigan

Published by Baker Books
a division of Baker Publishing Group
PO Box 6287, Grand Rapids, MI 49516-6287
www.bakerbooks.com

Printed in the United States of America

Library of Congress Cataloging-in-Publication Data
Names: Pokluda, Jonathan, 1980– author.
Title: Welcome to adulting : navigating faith, friendship, finances, and the future /
    Jonathan "JP" Pokluda with Kevin McConaghy.
Description: Grand Rapids : Baker Publishing Group, 2018. | Includes
    bibliographical references and index.
Identifiers: LCCN 2018008438 | ISBN 9780801078101 (pbk. : alk. paper)
Subjects: LCSH: Young adults—Religious life. | Christian life.
Classification: LCC BV4529.2 .P65 2018 | DDC 248.8/4—dc23
LC record available at https://lccn.loc.gov/2018008438

The author is represented by The Gates Group of 1403 Walnut Lane, Louisville, Kentucky 40223

In keeping with biblical principles of creation stewardship, Baker Publishing Group advocates the responsible use of our natural resources. As a member of the Green Press Initiative, our company uses recycled paper when possible. The text paper of this book is composed in part of post-consumer waste.

19   20   21   22   23   24   7

To my wife, Monica,

for patiently adulting with me.

To Christ-following young adults,

you are the future of the church.

The future is bright!

To our church, Watermark,

and the leaders there,

thank you

for displaying Christ

to me.

Contents

Introduction   9

SECTION ONE:
ADULTING WITH PURPOSE

1. Life: *Don't Miss It*   15
2. Purpose: *The Reason You're Here*   25

SECTION TWO:
ADULTING LIKE A BOSS

3. Authority: *Who's in Charge Here?*   39
4. Work: *Career Counseling*   55
5. Money: *It's Not All about the Benjamins*   71

SECTION THREE:
ADULTING WITH FRIENDS

6. Community: *Your Playmates and Playgrounds*   93
7. Conflict: *The Right Way to Be Wrong (and Vice Versa)*   111
8. Dating: *Happily Ever After?*   125

SECTION FOUR:
ADULTING FEARLESSLY

9. Worry: *The Only Thing We Have to Fear* . . .   159

10. Recovery: *Leaving the Past Behind*   173

SECTION FIVE:
ADULTING FOREVER

11. Eternity: *Life in Perspective*   191

Acknowledgments   213

Notes   215

About the Author   221

Introduction

*adulting (noun; mass noun informal): the practice of behaving in a way characteristic of a responsible adult, especially the accomplishment of mundane but necessary tasks.

I had just walked across the stage in my cap and gown in Waco, Texas. Not at Baylor, the Baptist university you might have heard of, but at a small technical college just outside of Waco. My girlfriend came in from out of town. She was sitting beside my proud parents, who drove across the state of Texas to witness the occasion. They had financed the possibility of graduation over the years, and I'm confident the event meant much more to them than it did to me. In fact, I was a little distracted from the diploma I was holding, because sitting behind my girlfriend was another girl I had been secretly dating in Waco. And she had driven over with another girl whom I was also interested in. So my mind was stuck on how I was going to keep those two away from my girlfriend while still appropriately expressing appreciation to everyone for coming to my graduation. This "mess" was a microcosm of my life.

My mother was a school counselor, and she was the one who had found this technical college where they would teach me about graphic art and help me find a job upon graduation. Well, today was that day, and I was still waiting tables at Johnny Carino's with no other job opportunities in sight. I didn't mind it, though. Having to do art for a grade in all those classes pretty much taught me to hate art. Now that I was finished with college, I still wasn't any closer to knowing what I wanted to do. I imagined I would do just about anything, as long as the job paid me enough money so that I could eat and party.

My life at this point was nearly void of faith. I went to a Catholic school from kindergarten through the eighth grade, and during sober nights in college (which were the exception) I'd usually go to sleep saying the prayers I had learned there. Outside of that, God and I were at odds. It wasn't his fault, it was mine. I spent college doing whatever I wanted, whenever I wanted. Sometimes that included going to class and sometimes it didn't. It never, however, included going to church.

Somehow, though, I had made it to this day. The last day I would ever have to attend school. The first day of the rest of my life. All I could think about, other than managing my relationship problems in the audience, was *Now what? What am I going to do now?*

It's been sixteen years since that day, and my life has taken some very interesting twists and turns. I've gone from small-town kid to big-city adult, gotten married, become a father, and worked my way through several jobs. The most unexpected plot twist is what I do now: I'm a pastor at a large church (Watermark Community Church in Dallas). There, I lead The Porch ministry—a weekly gathering of thousands of young adults, both in Dallas and through live-stream services around the world. With over a decade of ministering to tens of thousands of young adults, I've learned so much about what some do to succeed at this crossroads and how some fail. Besides having my own experiences as a young adult, including making mistakes and having failures to learn from, I've also walked alongside and counseled literally thousands of other people in their twenties or early thirties. I've seen what works and what doesn't work, what brings happiness and what brings pain. I've had the opportunity to study the Scriptures and to be mentored by Bible experts older and wiser than I am, and I have seen how following (or ignoring) God's wisdom leads to very different outcomes in life.

Through it all, I've found that these young professionals and recent graduates are almost all asking the same question I was. *Now what?* Some of them are asking a more hopeless version of that question: *Is this really it? Is this all there is?* I've learned that college, and school in general, doesn't prepare anyone for life's biggest challenges. The darkest days for many are those years following college. This is where someone goes from the one routine they'd known since age five—attending classes, obeying teachers, and taking tests—to another routine that is full of a freedom no one is really ready for.

I believe the pages ahead will help you plan for the rest of your life. You might think it's arrogant that I could claim to know the plan for your life. However, what I've realized is that God has a plan for everyone's life, but most people ignore it. They know the basic things God wants everyone to do, but they choose not to do them. And if you ignore the general plan God has already made clear, why should he bother to give you more specific instructions? But when we choose to walk in his basic plan for our life, we can unlock his greatest plan for our life.

The following chapters provide a sort of map. They cover the biggest challenges that I see young adults facing in the real world. Whether you were a valedictorian with a perfect GPA or felt that classes only got in the way of your college experience, I believe you will benefit greatly from the contents of this book. My hope is that this will be one of the greatest gifts you've ever received because of how it prepares you for the next season of life and saves you from the pain of the mistakes that many make at this crossroads.

I hope you don't read this book alone. While you could do so and still benefit from it, I've written this book so you can discuss the chapters with a small group of people who know you well and who are working through the book alongside you. I believe the discussion will help the ideas sink in and help you plan to make any necessary changes to your life.

Adulting
with
Purpose

1
Life

DON'T MISS IT

"I've tested the warnings of God and found them true. Now, I am trusting his promises."[1] I heard someone say that once, and it resonated deeply with me. To trust the promises of God is to live life as it is meant to be lived. It's an adventure with purpose. Faith is not a by-product of life; it *is* life, as it was meant to be lived. It seems most of my life I've been asking:

What is life all about?

I grew up on a farm in South Texas. We lived on twenty acres outside a small town of six thousand people in the middle of nowhere. I often describe my childhood as an extended identity crisis. People usually respond to that with, "It's normal to try to figure out who you are as a child." I get that. However, I was a member of Future Farmers of

America, an agricultural program in our school, and I showed hogs, sheep, and cattle competitively. Unlike your typical "future farmer," though, I also had my ears pierced, got my first tattoo at fifteen, rode a skateboard, and drove a 1979 Mercedes Benz with a sticker on the rear windshield that read "Superfly." That was me: your superfly future farmer. I was very involved in church—three churches, actually—but I was sometimes high when I was there.

Like I said: identity crisis. I had no idea who I wanted to be. And that continued beyond my childhood, when I was officially supposed to start adulting.

College was a blur of parties, girls, and fights, with classes mixed in there somewhere. Somehow I graduated and found myself in the big city of Dallas, Texas. As a twentysomething first setting out on this journey called adulthood, I wanted it all. I was on a search for stuff, status, and success. You only live once, right? And I wanted to make the most of it.

Money? I went from one sales job to another, looking for a bigger paycheck. I sold everything from clothes to gym memberships to real estate, until I landed in the highest-paying job I could find, which was being a global account manager for a large telecom company. I spent the money I made on clothes, watches, cars, and a high-rise condo in Uptown. I thought I was rich.

Success? I worked hard to climb the corporate ladder and managed to make it up a few rungs. I craved respect and power. I wanted to be important and be treated as someone important.

Women? From the fifth grade on, I was never without a girlfriend. Most of those relationships overlapped; I'd start seeing someone new before breaking up with my existing girlfriend, a strategy more commonly known as "cheating." As an adult, I went from one one-night stand to another and usually had a girlfriend on the side. I thought the real goal of dating was pleasure. Of course, I didn't have to have a real woman for that. I was also addicted to online pornography, just like pretty much every other guy I knew.

Fun? Of course I went after fun. For me, that usually involved some excuse to be stupid, such as drinking and drugs. Bars were fun. Bottle service was fun. Parties were fun. Even getting outdoors and going to the lake was fun, primarily because I could sit on a boat with friends and get drunk.

In all of that, my goal was to enjoy life. To be happy. And it worked, sort of. It just didn't last. The happiness didn't stay. I was getting what I thought I wanted from life, but it continued to leave me feeling discontented. It's kind of like when I was a kid and really wanted a remote-controlled car I'd seen on a commercial at Christmastime. Do you remember really wanting a particular gift? When Christmas came around and I actually got the exact gift I wanted, I was happy—for a couple of hours. That's about how long it took for the excitement to wear off, and for me to realize this greatest-toy-ever wasn't really as much fun as they made it look on TV. I'd been lied to.

That's what the world does. It lies to you. I had searched for significance in the wrong things and only realized that after having them and still coming up empty.

The Lake House

I spent a few years in the dull cycle of working all week and living for the weekend. We'd start partying on Thursday, so that the weekend could last longer, and basically did the same things every time. Wash, rinse, repeat. It wasn't very creative and soon ceased to be that interesting. I chased away boredom with the next thrill, but boredom continued to find me.

One typical Saturday night, I was at a bar on Lower Greenville, the center of Dallas's party scene. There I ran into an old friend I hadn't seen in a while. I asked what she was up to that weekend, and she unexpectedly responded that she would be visiting a church the next day. "Great," I said. "My church sucks. Pick me up."

At that time, I went to church only on occasion. For me, it was a place where I daydreamed for an hour and occasionally asked for forgiveness for the events from the previous night. That girl did pick me up the next morning, and the church she took me to seemed different. I started going there regularly and began to make friends there. Soon, a few of those new friends invited me to join them at their lake house for a weekend.

I was used to spending weekends at the lake. As I drove out there, I had a couple hours in the car to think. I wondered what it would be like to go to the lake with "church friends." I pulled up to the lake house as the other guys had just finished playing golf. I took note that none of them were drinking. That was a different kind of golf than I was used to, and it didn't sound fun. As the evening started, I also noticed that there were no girls. I knew it would be a guys' trip, but when I had been on guys' trips before, usually our objective was to get girls there or talk about the last time we were with girls. Here there wasn't even a conversation about girls.

Most of these men were happily married. Some of them were very successful. I couldn't help but notice the size of the lake house. A three-story lakefront home, with cathedral ceilings, big-screen TVs, and million-dollar finish-out. It was something I could only dream of affording someday. But nobody seemed to care about that; everyone treated everyone else (including me) as equals.

That night was extraordinary to me. We began the evening by grilling steaks, and after an incredible meal, we played poker. I don't think we even played for money, but I can't remember. The game was just an excuse to talk. We had meaningful conversations, not the normal drunken-slurred talk I was accustomed to. We talked about changing the world, and I was convinced that the men at the table could pull off the plans they had.

One of the guys was a pastor. But he wasn't the normal over-polished, posing kind of pastor I had seen before. He would hold the attention of the other guys there. He wasn't careful and guarded with his words—but he also wasn't reckless. He was just real. He asked me thought-provoking questions. Questions about why we were there and what life was really about. That pastor was Todd Wagner of Watermark, who has since become my dear friend and mentor. We talked, we ate, we played cards, and we literally laughed until we cried several times over. I couldn't believe how much fun I was having!

That night I couldn't sleep. I couldn't reconcile the joy I had just experienced when it was so different than my usual weekend activities. It seemed to be a normal time together for these men, but it was different for me. There was a depth and purpose to what had just happened. It was so much better than what I was used to. I couldn't help but wonder if I had been doing life all wrong. I couldn't help but wonder if I had been missing it.

I laid awake all night in the bottom bunk in an oversized room, deep in thought and in and out of prayer. I left early the next morning, and I called my best friend, Matt, as soon as I thought he would be awake. But since he had been partying the night before, I ended up waking him up. Matt answered the phone in a groggy voice and asked me if everything was OK, and I told him it had never been better. I hadn't even slept but I felt great. I didn't feel guilty or have the foggy feeling of a hangover. I told Matt we had been missing out on life.

Don't Miss It

The purpose of this book is to make sure you don't miss it.

Unfortunately, most people do. They spend years, or sometimes their entire lives, pursuing things that don't ultimately bring life. And it's more than just a waste of valuable time; these pursuits usually end up causing real pain, both to themselves and the people they are close to. I know that pain well, through my own life and the lives I've observed from leading in ministry.

Why do so many people get it wrong? Well, we've been sold a lie that sets us up for failure. The world, the media, and even our own internal desires tell us that the way to be happy is to pursue things like money, sex, fame, power, and material possessions. The United States' economy is even built around it. Fact is, we have more of these things than anyone in the history of the world before us. We're richer, we have more cool stuff, and we have the ability to do almost anything we want with almost anyone we want and not even be judged for it. Yet studies show we're statistically less happy and more depressed than ever before.[2] We've pursued happiness and found ourselves sadder than any generation that has ever lived.

Some people eventually figure it out, but only after many years of making poor decisions and seeing the consequences that come from that. Experience is a hard teacher, and its main lesson is regret. Though it's never too late to change, it is also never too early. And far too often, the longer you wait, the more difficult change is.

Maybe you've been reading and waiting for the moment in my story when I "get what I have coming." Maybe you've kept all the rules and can't wait to see what happens to someone who has broken them. Well, you don't win, either. You're no better off than the drunks or the prostitutes. Your self-righteousness has kept you from finding life as it was intended, and at some point in your journey with Jesus, you've found yourself in maintenance mode. Not doing anything too bad—but not doing anything too good either. As you read, I hope you find a reset button for your adulting journey.

This is why I spend so much time around young adults who have recently come to understand what God desires for them. These people are just setting out in the world, leaving behind the structure of parents and school and becoming fully responsible for the direction of their lives. It's a unique time, because life is still an empty canvas stretching out in front of them, and they get to choose where to go and what to do with it. It's a point where every decision, and every action, can have a huge impact—either good or bad. Choices here are more important than they are at any other time in their lives. But it's also the first time they've gotten to make such decisions, so they're not very good at it yet.

That's why I'm trying to help—and also partly because of my own experiences and the things I wish I had done differently. Though my life now has completely changed (and I'll tell you how), I still had to work through some consequences, and I'd like to spare you from that. Learn from my mistakes.

Beyond just avoiding some negative consequences, I want you to find life and experience it to the fullest (John 10:10)! I cannot tell you how amazing it is to begin to live your life as God intended it to be lived. When you wake up and know you have been placed in time and space for a purpose, you begin to realize that every aspect of your life matters. You begin to see yourself as part of the solution to the problems you see in the world. There is something inside all of us that desires to be a vigilante superhero like Batman—fighting evil and doing good. I have seen young adults get this and begin to make war with evil, not outside the law but within it.

Besides my own life, I've been able to observe the lives of thousands of young adults over the past decade or so that I've been in full-time young adult ministry. I've celebrated and served alongside people who have gotten it right and counseled those dealing with the aftermath of getting it wrong. I've seen what consistently works and what never ever seems to work. Most importantly, I've been able to study what the Creator has to say about how to live a full life, which—no surprise—matches up with the results I've seen in today's world. So many of these young adults have traded in the American Dream for something much better. They are changing the world, saving lives, solving problems, and making a difference.

Hopefully, this can serve as a kind of how-to book: how to "adult," how to navigate through life, and how to live a life that really matters.

Reflection

- What is the most fun you've ever had?
- When have you really looked forward to something only to find yourself disappointed after it actually occurred?
- Where have you been "missing it"?
- What changes would you like to make in your life?

2
Purpose

THE REASON YOU'RE HERE

A few years ago, an online video clip from a German TV show went viral. In it, a grown woman and her elder dad are in the kitchen cooking something. As her dad chops vegetables in the background, the woman asks him if he'd gotten a chance to try out any of the apps on the new iPad she'd given him. "What's an app?" he replies, as he brings the chopped vegetables over to the stove—and we see that he's been using the iPad as a cutting board. As his daughter looks on in shock, he scrapes the vegetables into a pot with his knife, rinses off the dirty iPad in the sink, and nonchalantly places it in the dishwasher.

It's funny, but it's also kind of painful to watch, especially if you're a gadget person (or merely familiar with how much a new iPad is worth). It shouldn't really matter; I mean, it's his iPad, and he's free to use it however he wants. Though

I haven't tried it, an iPad would probably work fairly well as a cutting board, if that's what you really wanted to use it for. But it bothers people, and gets a reaction, because that's not what it's designed to do.

Now, imagine if the scene were replayed, but instead of an iPad he was using a professional-grade cutting board made from some exotic type of wood. (Believe it or not, some such cutting boards can cost just as much as an iPad.) Now, no one would bat an eye at him cutting up vegetables on it or washing it off afterward. Nobody would have a problem with him doing that at all. That's because he'd be using something the way it was designed to be used. The cutting board would be fulfilling its purpose.

The Meaning of Life

Why am I here? What should I be doing? *What is the meaning of life?*

The question is so common, so universal, as to be a cliché. It's especially common in comic strips, for some reason, where it's normally portrayed as a person climbing to the peak of a tall mountain in order to ask the question to an old bearded man who's seated there. As if he'd know. Apparently, the meaning of life is to sit on top of a mountain.

There's even a Wikipedia page on the subject, which at the time of this writing has well over twelve thousand words (for comparison, the entry for "physics"—as in, the entire field of physics—has about six thousand words) and dozens of different answers to the question.

The point is, it's a question almost everyone asks at some point—and a question that, I would argue, you should ask.

Because, just like an iPad or a cutting board, your life does have a purpose. You were specially created and put here on this earth to do something. And if you spend your whole life and never fulfill your purpose, that's immensely more tragic than using an iPad to chop carrots. It would be a waste of a life. Your life.

What You're Created to Do

One funny thing about purpose is that you don't really get to decide what your own purpose is. The creator of an object decides its purpose.

Take the iPad, for example. An iPad doesn't decide whether it's designed to be a computer or a cutting board. The creator of the iPad chooses. The people who designed it first decided what they wanted it to be used for, and then created something that could fulfill that purpose. A computer without a keyboard or mouse? Then we'd better design it with a touchscreen. Something that can be used on the go? Better make it relatively small and light, and include a battery. Want it to include the ability to take pictures? Then we'll need to put a camera in there. It's intentionally designed to fulfill a set purpose.

The same is true for the cutting board: though you could use it as—I don't know, maybe a chunk of firewood—it's designed by its creator to be a cutting board. The bamboo or purple heart wood (that's a thing) was chosen by its creator because it is especially durable or water-resistant or has antibacterial properties.

Now, consider something that isn't designed or created by a human—like, say, your eyes. Clearly, their purpose is to enable you to see. They're completely useless for anything else, like chewing food or listening to music. And, again, they don't get to decide what their purpose is: it was determined by their creator. Ah—but who, or what, is their creator?

This is where your worldview comes in and becomes important. Some people have a worldview that says there is no creator. They believe that eyes are the product of naturalistic evolution: random mutations over a long period of time that were naturally selected to be passed down to offspring because they were useful and made it more likely that you *could* live long enough to produce offspring. If that were the case, then the eye would still be the product of design, with natural selection itself as the designer. The eye would still be designed to enable you to see, but only because seeing helps you survive long enough to produce offspring. That would be its purpose.

And that would be *your* purpose, as well: to live long enough to mate and pass on your genes to your offspring. That's it, in its entirety, if your worldview is that we're all here by random chance. Reproduction would be the sole reason why you were given eyes, a nose, a mouth, a brain, and everything else that comes with a standard-issue human body. Pretty simple, really.

Yet most everyone believes that their real purpose in life involves more than that. In my experience, even the people who deny that there is an intelligent creator usually still feel instinctively that there is a greater purpose for their lives. In fact, they often seem *more* likely to search for meaning and to try to define what it means to live a worthwhile life. They'll define the meaning of life as living morally or say that their purpose is to help their fellow humans. Never mind that sacrificially helping others, especially people you don't know, is a value that runs completely contrary to the principle of natural selection. It's great that you're helping feed a child in a third-world country—really, thank you for doing that—but that does nothing to pass down your own genes and it takes away resources that could be spent giving your own children a better life. What would be your motive for doing so? What would even determine what is and is not moral?

Although they might come up with something that *sounds* good, they're still just inventing a purpose that isn't there. It's like using an iPad as a cutting board, or using a cutting board as firewood: sure, you can make it work, but that's definitely not what it was designed for.

Here's the deal: I'm not saying your life doesn't have a distinct, worthwhile, noble purpose. In fact, I'm saying that it *does*, and I believe that purpose is greater and more fulfilling than you ever dared to imagine. But that's only possible because there is an intelligent Creator (capital "C") who designed you, specifically *you*, with a unique purpose in mind. Understanding that purpose will be key in living out your life correctly from here on out.

God's Will for You

The Bible is actually really clear in stating that God has a purpose for your life. For example, in Ephesians 2:10, it says:

> For we are God's handiwork, created in Christ Jesus to do good works, which God prepared in advance for us to do.

That word *handiwork* can also be translated as "masterpiece." We were created as intricately and carefully as fine works of art. Why were we created that way? To do good works. And not just good works in general, but things that God has specifically prepared in advance for us to do. He knows what's going to happen, and he's created you in a particular way and placed you at this exact moment in history to accomplish some specific good works. It's your job, so to speak; it's why you are here.

It's worth pointing out that these good works are not how you earn your way into heaven. That's made very clear when you look at the two verses immediately before verse 10: "For it is by grace you have been saved, through faith—and this is not from yourselves, it is the gift of God—not by works, so that no one can boast" (vv. 8–9). You're saved by grace, which is the free gift of Jesus paying for our sins on the cross, and not by any works you do, "so that no one can boast" that they were saved through their own merits or effort. But once you are saved, God has a role for you to play, and he lets you take part in his grand plan.

You may be thinking, *That's great—I have a God-given purpose. So what is it, exactly?* Let me ask: If I could tell you, would you live it?

For starters, there are some general things from Scripture that apply to everyone. The Great Commission, for instance, which states that we are to "go and make disciples" (Matt. 28:19). That means we are to replicate ourselves, teaching others what we have learned so they can later disciple yet more people (2 Tim. 2:2). That's why I hope you don't read this book alone. If you are, stop and invite others in. Read and discuss the ideas as a group.

The Bible also says that it's God's will for you to avoid committing obvious sins (1 Thess. 4:3–5; 1 Pet. 2:15–16;

4:2–3). Most sins are fairly clear-cut. You don't have to sit and puzzle over whether God wants you to lie or get drunk or have sex with somebody you aren't married to. He's already said what you're supposed to do in those cases. If God has stated clearly "do this" or "don't do that," and if you know those commands and willingly choose to ignore them, don't expect him to give you some special message about what you should major in or where you should live. If you aren't going to listen to what God has already said, why should he say anything else to you? Why would God make known to you his unrevealed will if you are not living out his revealed will?

Finding Your SHAPE

If you do have the general things down—you know you're supposed to make disciples, and you're not currently reveling in sin—then you may be waiting for me to talk about specifics. Like, how do you make disciples? What, specifically, should you do with your life? What should you be doing *right now*?

That I can't tell you. I can't tell you simply because I don't know who you are, and the specifics are different for each unique person. But I can tell you how to figure it out for yourself.

Remember the iPad example? Well, imagine that you knew nothing at all about tablet computers. You'd never seen one, or even heard about them. And then someone hands you an unlocked iPad. Would you be able to figure out its purpose? Of course you would. It might take some time, but by playing around with it and trying different things you'd eventually figure out what it was designed to do. Even my four-year-old, who doesn't know how to read or write, has figured out how to use my iPad.

It's not all that much different with people. If you want to know what you're created for, start by looking at how you're created. What are you good at? What do you most enjoy doing? What things are you able to master quickly, while other people struggle to do them? What makes you unique?

Pastor Rick Warren uses the acrostic S.H.A.P.E. when talking about this process of learning about how you've been uniquely created.[1] The letters stand for five different aspects of yourself that you should look at.

Spiritual Gifts

God gives spiritual gifts to each believer. Different gifts are listed in 1 Corinthians 12 and Romans 12:6–8. Potential gifts include teaching, serving, giving, leadership, administration, and wisdom, among others. Every Christ-follower is given at least one spiritual gift.

How do you know which gift or gifts you've been given? Basically, you have to try them and see. If you have a gift, that means you will be gifted at doing that particular thing. You'll be relatively good at it, and likely have other people comment on the fact that you seem good at it. Today, there are also spiritual gift tests that you can take online, though they mostly ask questions related to what you're good at and what other people say you're good at.

Is it easy for you to talk to strangers about spiritual topics? You might have the gift of evangelism. Do you enjoy reading and explaining the Bible? You might have the gift of teaching. Do you enjoy having people over and making sure they are well cared for and comfortable? You could have the gift of hospitality. You get the picture. God has given you gifts to serve him with. Do you know what they are?

Heart

Heart refers to what you care about or feel passionately about. For example, some people, like my wife, may have a heart for working with children. They really care about teaching children, or making sure that kids everywhere are cared for. Other people may not feel that strongly about kids but have a heart for the elderly instead.

These are just examples; there are many causes you could have a heart for. If you care deeply about something that God also cares about, that's likely an area where you should deploy your gifts.

Abilities

We're all good at something. It could be a natural talent, or it could be something we've studied and worked hard to develop. Either way, your abilities define what you can do at this point in time.

For example, I have some friends who are really good at music. Like, recording-contract good. They use those gifts to lead worship at church, write songs, perform at concerts, and support their families. It makes sense for them to use that ability they've developed over a lifetime of practice. I *don't* have that kind of musical ability. I'm not saying I'm terrible at it, but I'm just nowhere near as good as they are. So it makes sense for me to let them handle the music stuff, while I work at something that utilizes my own abilities.

Personality

We've probably all taken a personality test at some point. They can tell you whether you're extroverted or introverted, whether you like order or thrive in chaos, or whether you enjoy taking risks or prefer playing it safe. There's no right or wrong personality, but your unique personality can make you better suited for some roles than others.

Experiences

Everyone is shaped at least partly by their past. We all have a mix of good and bad experiences—some better and some worse than others. These experiences influence what you're good at doing, what you care about most, and maybe even your personality. They also allow you to relate to, understand, or give advice to other people who have been through (or are currently going through) similar experiences.

This is where God often works to bring something good out of something that was once bad. Almost every ministry I can think of was started because of someone's experiences. A man who struggled with addiction starts a twelve-step recovery ministry. A woman who had an abortion and thought she could never speak of it gets the courage to tell someone about her decision, and God uses her to start an abortion recovery ministry. A man who went to prison starts a prison outreach ministry. I could go on and on for pages. Any mistake you've made, or any bad thing that someone has done to you, God can use for good (Gen. 50:20). Such things don't disqualify you from making a difference; they're actually what makes you qualified. You know *exactly* what someone else is going through, because you've been through it yourself. You can relate. You know what to say, and you can get them to listen. In the gospel, God has taken your mess and made it your message.

---∞∞∞---

In other words, your SHAPE tells you what you are naturally good at, what you want to do, what you're able to do, how you like to do it, and what you know a lot about. Put them all together, find where they intersect, and you'll find something that you were created to do.

For example, I've been given the spiritual gifts of leadership and teaching. I have a heart for young adults, because of how important that life stage is and because I've seen for myself what can happen if you make the wrong choices (or the right ones). I have some ability at public speaking, partly because I started my career focused on sales jobs and took classes to get better at giving presentations to prospective clients. I have a bit of an extroverted personality, so I enjoy being around people and helping them. And I have the experience of making most of the classic young adult mistakes, meaning I can relate to and empathize with other people who make those same mistakes. Put that together, and it makes perfect sense that I would spend over a decade leading a young adult gathering. God planned for me to do that all along.

What about you? Are you a teacher, an engineer, an administrator, a strategic thinker? How can your SHAPE help you understand what you were meant to do today? For example, are you more introverted than extroverted? If so, alone time is going to be very important for you to be able to love others. My wife comes alive when she finds a rhythm of stillness and alone time. Her spiritual gifts lean toward showing mercy to others. Her heart is for those who need help. And as I said, she is extremely skilled with children, in training them and caring for them. While she recharges by herself, she is the single best lover of people I know.

You can have more than one intersection of your gifts, abilities, experiences, and so on. There are other things I do, such as being a husband and father, that are just as important as my day job. These are ministries too. So you can have more than just one purpose. And things like your abilities and experiences can change over time, which means God may have you focus on different things in different stages of your life. It's an ongoing adventure.

By doing what you're created to do—what you're good at, what you're passionate about, what you have experience in—you'll naturally be more successful at it. You'll make a bigger impact for God's kingdom, and you won't get tired of it or burn out as easily. And you won't waste what you've been given. It will be the best use of your life.

Reflection

- What are your spiritual gifts, passions, abilities, and personality, and what experiences have shaped your journey?
- What are you certain your purpose is as it is revealed in Scripture?
- What special tasks do you think God might have created you to do?
- What prevents you from fully living out your purpose?

Adulting Like a Boss

3
Authority

WHO'S IN CHARGE HERE?

I laid in my twin-sized bed, in my on-campus apartment, weeping. I had been in college for less than one month, and this wasn't how I saw it going.

I wasn't homesick. I wasn't sad because of something that had happened to me. I was devastated because of the choices I had made. The last three weeks had been marked by me doing everything I wanted to do. Attending every party I wanted to attend. Sleeping with every girl I wanted to sleep with. College for me meant "freedom at last."

Unfortunately, I didn't have the maturity to handle that freedom, and I found myself in a pit of sadness. As I prayed, it seemed my prayers were bouncing off the ceiling. The next day, I reached out for help to someone who gave me some terrible advice. They said, "That's just what college is. You have fun and then you grow up afterward."

Growing Up

As kids, we all dream of growing up. Every single one of us looks forward to the day we can move out of our parents' house, finally be done with school, or finally be out on our own.

But why is that? It's not like being a kid is so tough. We don't have to pay rent, we don't have to work for a living, and most of us have very few responsibilities. We may worry about passing the next algebra test or how well we'll perform on the JV team, but that's nothing compared to the stresses of getting a job, keeping a job, paying bills, and trying to make ends meet. When you think about it, being a kid sounds like a pretty good gig.

But there is one big difference between being a kid and being an adult that seems to outweigh all of those things. It is, as near as I can tell, the one and only reason why kids and teenagers and college students all look forward to being a full-fledged adult.

What is that one thing that outweighs everything else?

Freedom.

As an adult, you're finally in charge of your own life. You're not subject to an educational authority, having to make certain grades and learn certain things and jump through certain hoops to get a diploma. You're no longer under the authority of your parents, or at least no more than you choose to be. No one's telling you to brush your teeth, or clean up your room, or go to bed at a certain time. Now you're the head of the household, and you get to make your own rules.

That's a good thing—and it's a bad thing.

It's a good thing because that really is a key part of being an adult. With freedom comes responsibility; if you're in charge of making a decision, you're responsible for what happens as a result of that decision. In a way, being responsible is what being an adult is all about.

But that same freedom can be a bad thing if it becomes your ultimate thing. Some people don't want anyone telling them what to do. Ever. They rebel against authority. They refuse to listen to sound advice. They avoid getting into situations or relationships where someone even *could* have authority over them or give them advice, so they don't have to hear it.

Really, I'm talking about all of us here, at least at certain times. I'm definitely talking about myself; I have a problem with authority sometimes. I want to be in charge. I don't want anyone telling me what to do.

That's an issue because, like it or not, we are all under authority. It's not only how things are; it's how things are *supposed* to be. It's the way God intends it. And since you are under authority, when you rebel against that authority, things will not go well with you.

The Authority Problem

Rebelling against authority isn't a new problem; it's the oldest problem. It's what happened in the Garden of Eden, when the first humans chose to disobey the one restriction that had been placed on them. They didn't trust the one in authority (God), thought they knew better than he did about what was best for them, and felt that perhaps they should be in charge instead (they wanted to "be like God" [Gen. 3:5]).

Things aren't much different today. We still wonder whether we should trust those who are in authority. We think we know better than they do about what's best for us. We want to be in charge instead.

But this generation seems to have a bigger problem with authority than most. Partly it's because, as young adults, you're still generally at the lower end of the totem pole. You don't have seniority in anything. You're usually not the boss or the leader. Some of you may even be coming out of school organizations and student leadership positions, where you did have some semblance of authority, only to find that now you're essentially the incoming freshmen pledges of the real world.

That's always been the case for young adults, but today some people go much further in questioning authority. We often see people rebelling against the fundamental concepts of right and wrong. I don't mean that they disagree about what's right and what's wrong; I mean they reject the idea that "right" and "wrong" even exist. It's convenient for them, because if there is no right and wrong, then nobody can tell them to do or not do anything. However, denying an authority doesn't make the authority go away. It just leads to the consequences that come from rebelling against that authority.

It does not take much time or creativity to think about how we rebel against authorities of all types.

For some people, the consequence of seeking freedom from authority is that you lose the very freedom you crave. Want to live in a place where every single resident has a problem with authority and has chosen not to let that authority interfere with what they wanted to do or how they wanted to live their lives? Such a place exists. It's called *prison.*

You don't have to be literally locked up for your freedom to turn into a prison. There are far more people who wanted nothing more than the freedom to pursue alcohol, drugs, pornography, or some other vice. By consuming more and more of it, they eventually lost the freedom to say no to it. That's what an addiction is: a loss of freedom. They can't stop pursuing the very thing they wanted the freedom to pursue.

Another place I see this sort of imprisonment is often when I engage with the homeless to see how I can best meet their needs. I start by getting to know them, and that always involves a conversation. I have loved hearing their stories and reminding them that they are loved and are people created in God's image with dignity. However, one of the sad patterns I've realized through these conversations is that often they are people who have wanted to be free their entire lives. Not free from homelessness but free from authority, which in some cases can lead to homelessness. I do not intend to simplify a complex problem like homelessness or stereotype those in this situation. Again, I'm just speaking from some of my own interactions. Some of the people I've talked to have rebelled against authorities, invited in addictions, and found themselves to be some of the most "free" people on the planet. They sleep where they want. Go where they want. And do much of what they want.

None of us, however, would look with envious eyes on the freedom homelessness offers. At times, when I've offered to help and have pointed them to some of our ministry partners, many have refused to go there, stating they don't like the strict rules like curfews, mandatory classes, or substance abuse policies. Their desire for freedom has led them into a routine of imprisonment.

True Freedom

I too have experienced that cycle of imprisonment. When I became an adult, I wanted total freedom. Freedom from rules. Freedom from anybody telling me what to do. I wanted to have my own kingdom; my goal was to accumulate enough money and enough power so that nobody could tell me what to do. This is what freedom looked like to me.

But that's not what God says freedom looks like.

To be clear, if you are a Christian, the Bible definitely teaches that we are free. I know many people view Christianity as a long set of rules to follow that are seemingly designed to restrict freedom. But that's not the case. Christ-followers should be the freest people on the face of the earth. Jesus said that "the truth will set you free," and "if the Son sets you free, you will be free indeed" (John 8:32, 36). Because salvation is a free gift, those of us who have accepted that gift are set free from having to do anything to earn God's approval. We're even set free from the power of death (Rom. 8:1–2), which is sort of like ignoring the biggest rule of all. Everybody has to die? Meh. No thanks. I'll just come back in a new body and live forever.

As we are living out that freedom, though, the Bible is quite specific about how we are to handle the question of authority. Not because it's a rule to follow but because things will not go well for us if we rebel against those God has placed in authority.

And there are three earthly, human authorities that adults are asked to submit to: the government, employers, and the church.

The Government

Yeah, *government* is not a very popular one. The most recent poll I've seen says that only 20 percent of Americans trust the federal government most or all of the time, which means four-fifths of the US population does not trust the government (the one *they* elected) most of the time.[1] Though poll numbers go up and down a little over time, this particular measure has been pretty consistently negative for most of the past forty years. And I'm saying Christians are supposed to submit to *that*?

Yes. That's what the Bible says, anyway.

> Submit yourselves for the Lord's sake to every human authority: whether to the emperor, as the supreme authority, or to governors, who are sent by him to punish those who do wrong and to commend those who do right. (1 Pet. 2:13–14)

We may not have an "emperor" today, but we do have a president who, along with the rest of the federal government, represents the "supreme authority" of our country. We do have "governors," and an entire legal/judicial system that the government uses to "punish those who do wrong."

So what does it mean to submit to the government? Basically, you obey the laws. You don't murder, you don't steal from anybody, you use your turn signal, you pay your taxes. If you don't follow the law, the consequences can be harsh.

But, you might ask, what if the laws aren't fair? What if our government leaders are wicked or corrupt? Well, first and foremost, *work to change that*. You have a vote; use it. Get involved. Campaign for better laws. Some of you, at some point, should probably run for office and be the godly leaders we desperately need. And all of us should pray for our elected officials, asking that they would govern wisely and uphold the freedoms we're supposed to have.

If, by law, you are asked to do something that goes directly against one of God's commands, that's when you would disobey the government and obey the higher authority (God). But, although there are many laws that *allow* things that go against God's Word, there are (so far) very few that might require you to do something evil. Let's work to try to prevent any such laws.

No matter how bad you may think our government is, and how unworthy it is of your respect, it's still better than what Peter was dealing with when he wrote that people should submit to the government. His emperor at the time was Nero. Nero wouldn't have had very good approval ratings. Even his mother wasn't a big fan, so he had her killed. He also killed his first wife (who happened to be his stepsister) and had his stepbrother poisoned. After his second wife died (also possibly killed by Nero), he married a young boy, had him castrated, dressed him up like a woman, and called him by his dead wife's name. Nero also had a bad habit of burning Christians alive. He eventually had Peter killed on an upside-down cross—the same Peter who wrote this passage about submitting to the emperor.[2] My point: if people in Peter's time were told to submit to *that* government leader, surely it applies to whatever government leaders we have today.

Employers

A God who loves us also says that we are to submit to the authority of our employers. Unless you're self-employed or unemployed, this applies to you.

Now, when the Bible talks about employee-employer relationships, it doesn't use those words. Instead, it usually talks about "slaves" and "masters." Obviously, considering what we know about slavery today, or slavery in this country two hundred years ago, those terms raise some big red flags. But we need to understand that the Bible is talking about slavery not from two hundred years ago but from two thousand years ago. And in that time, slavery was quite different from the picture we usually think of today.

For starters, in New Testament times slavery was not specifically based on race. Anyone could be a slave. And it wasn't necessarily a lifelong thing; people could be slaves for a set number of years, after which they would be free (Exod. 21:2; Deut. 15:12–15).[3]

Slavery was also, at least part of the time, *voluntary*.[4] People sometimes chose to become slaves. Why would anyone choose to be a slave, you might ask? Because, again, we're talking about a different kind of slavery. People chose to become slaves because it was a form of employment. In a world where many people struggled just to afford food, clothing, and shelter, slavery provided all of those things in exchange for work.[5]

Also remember that the world wasn't run by big corporations back then. A job fair wouldn't have had very many booths. Most people were either self-employed (like Joseph the carpenter or Paul the tentmaker) or worked in the family business (James and John worked with their dad, Zebedee, as fishermen). If you weren't working for yourself or for a member of your family, the odds are pretty good that you were a slave. As weird as it sounds to say it, slavery is basically the closest Bible-times equivalent we have to working for a corporation today.[6]

So what does the Bible have to say about how you should treat your employer?

Slaves, in reverent fear of God submit yourselves to your masters, not only to those who are good and considerate, but also to those who are harsh. (1 Pet. 2:18)

There's that other uncomfortable "s" word: *submit*. Anticipating your objection to the command, Peter makes it clear that he's talking not only about submitting to good bosses "but also to those who are harsh." Bad employers are a reality. Though today you have the freedom to seek out a different employer if you don't like the one you have, you should still fulfill your role of being a good employee as long as you are working for them.

This is an area where today's generation of young adults has gotten kind of a bad reputation.[7] Bosses complain that young workers show no respect. New employees instantly want to be in charge and don't understand why they have to pay their dues and earn their way up the ladder.[8] Which is why our generation is also known for leaving: we jump into a job, until it gets difficult, and then we jump to another job, until it gets difficult . . . wash, rinse, repeat.[9] We get good at selling ourselves in the job interview, and then we're not very good at follow-through when the job gets difficult.

The next chapter will talk more about work, so suffice it to say: things will go better for you if you submit to the authority of your employer. Read on to find out why.

The Church

In my experience, the *church* category probably provides the most striking difference in how people view authority today, compared to older generations. Young adults are very unwilling to submit to the authority of a church.

I'm not talking about nonbelievers here. Of course they wouldn't be concerned with joining a church. I'm talking about believers, or those who claim to be followers of Christ. The majority of these people choose not to be under the authority of a church.

According to a 2014 Pew Research Center study, 80 to 84 percent of young adults believe in God, yet only 27 to 28 percent attend weekly religious services. (This includes people of all faiths, not just Christians, but Christians make up the vast majority of "believers" in the survey.) Another study by the Barna Research Group found that one out of six people don't attend just one church but hop around through a carefully chosen handful of churches on a rotating basis. This means that even though they are "regularly attending" services, they're not a regular member at any one church. It's a pattern that seems specifically designed to avoid getting too involved at any one church, and/or prevents people from getting to know you well enough that they can start to speak into how you're living your life. A separate 2015 Barna survey seems to confirm that Millennials avoid being truly known at church: two-thirds refused to share any contact info when visiting a church, and 18 percent wouldn't even share their first name.

There's also the rise of "spiritual but not religious," a popular survey answer that sounds kind of godly in a "relationship, not religion" kind of way, but is generally code for "I don't go to church." About 30 percent of young adults claim the "spiritual but not religious" tag, which means they have no ties to any "religious" authority. (By the way, the number of young adults who are "spiritual but not religious" has increased 50 percent in just the past five years. Five years ago, it was one out of five young adults; today, it is almost one out of three.)[10]

What's wrong with that? Aren't we supposed to be under the authority of God alone? *What's more, didn't you, JP, already say that "religion" doesn't work and that you're not "religious"?* Again, it depends on what you mean by "religion" or "religious."

There's a difference between impersonal, works-based acts of "religion" and having a personal relationship with other believers within a local church. And the biggest difference is this: the Holy Spirit, through the author of Hebrews, tells us to gather together regularly with other believers (Heb. 10:24–25), which is basically the definition of a "church."

If you want God to be your sole authority, please consider this: God, in his authority, has clearly said that you should submit yourself to the authority of church leadership.

> Remember your leaders, who spoke the word of God to you. Consider the outcome of their way of life and imitate their faith. . . . Have confidence in your leaders and submit to their

authority, because they keep watch over you as those who must give an account. Do this so that their work will be a joy, not a burden, for that would be of no benefit to you. (Heb. 13:7, 17)

Our generation sometimes seems to think we know better than God's Word. We say things like "You don't have to go to church to be a Christian." But I have seen the lives of thousands of young adults, and I have yet to see a single one of them who has grown in their relationship with Christ apart from belonging to a church. Please don't think that you will be the exception. A Christian is someone who follows Christ. To follow Christ is to belong to his body, the church, of which he is the head (Col. 1:18).

The reasons people rebel against submitting to the authority of the church are the same reasons people rebel against any authority. For some, it's a trust issue. Can we trust church leaders? After all, they are imperfect humans, just like us. They make mistakes. And a few high-profile church leaders have made the news with some very high-profile mistakes. *How do I know if they are steering me straight?*

That's a valid concern but also one that isn't very difficult to answer. All you have to do is compare their advice to what the Bible says. Do their teachings match up with Scripture? If so, then you're not only submitting to their authority but also obeying God's commands. If they clearly *don't* match up with Scripture, talk with the church leaders about it. Maybe they did make a mistake, and you can help them correct it. Or maybe they can help you better understand Scripture. Or maybe—and this does happen occasionally—they might be one of the false teachers the Bible warns about. If that's the case, you're still commanded to be under the church's authority; you just need to find a different church.

This doesn't mean you continually hop from church to church, though. If you've been to a half-dozen churches and decided they're *all* led by false teachers, the odds are starting to get pretty high that the problem lies with the common denominator: you. Perhaps you just want the Bible to mean something it doesn't and refuse to listen to teaching that disagrees with your own wants and desires. That's exactly the reason why we are supposed to submit to the authority of church leaders: so we can learn from them what the Bible really says.

And that relates to the other big reason some people rebel against church authority: they don't want to be told they're wrong. They don't want to change their ways or be challenged to follow God more closely. They don't want to have deep relationships with other Christians, because other Christians might point out things that they don't want to hear. I've heard it said, "If you find the perfect church, don't go there, because you'll ruin it." A healthy church is made up of imperfect people striving to be like Christ. We have a perfect Savior and we are his imperfect church.

All of us will make mistakes. Everyone will go astray at times. Unless you're perfect—which you're not—you will sometimes be wrong and need the wisdom of others to point that out. That way you won't go too far off track or stay in the wrong for too long. The local church is God's provision for you, to help you avoid the negative consequences that come from continuing the same mistakes.

If you question whether you *should* rebel against an authority in your life, such as an immoral law you need to disobey or a toxic boss you need to confront, your church community is also the best place to get biblically sound advice for how you should handle the situation. *Really?* you might be asking. Yes. A healthy, Bible-teaching church where you are known and cared for should help guide you to wisdom. If you don't belong to a place like this, I beg you to change that—for your own good.

Freedom under Authority

As I've mentioned, back in my twenties when I was so focused on my own freedom and building a kingdom of my own authority, someone at a bar invited me to church.

I sat, hungover, in the back row. I had a headache and still smelled like smoke from the club the night before. I hardly wanted to be at church, but that day I heard something that changed my life.

The preacher told a silly story about a horse. He was a wild stallion who just wanted to be free. I pictured the beast rearing up on a mountaintop, enjoying his freedom. *I can relate to that,* I thought. *I just want to be free. I want to be free to do whatever I want, whenever I want.* I was like this stallion.

He went on to talk about how the horse lived free in the wilderness but had to spend his days looking for food and water. He had no shelter from the wind, rain, and snow. And he lived in constant fear of being captured by someone. He didn't want anyone to take away his freedom.

One day, a cowboy successfully captured the wild stallion. He brought the wild horse home and took care of him. The cowboy spent time with the horse and eventually "broke" him, meaning he trained him to be ridden. As he rode him, he led the horse to lush pastures and clear streams for drinking.

He provided the horse with plenty of food, water, and protection from the elements.

As the pastor related the story, it was this line that changed my life: "It wasn't until he was fully submissive to his master that he truly found freedom." It wasn't just a silly story anymore. I realized I was seeking what I thought would bring freedom, but all it brought me was loneliness, broken relationships, addictions, and bad headaches.

Things didn't immediately change for me. It still took some convincing for me to submit to God's authority in my life, which included submitting to the earthly authorities he'd put over me. And there were some habits to break and fences to mend. Eventually, the words I used changed into words that built others up. The things I looked at were not perversions the world offered but things that led to life. What I did for fun changed to what didn't have consequences and only offered true enjoyment. Through the process, I've learned that the moral of that preacher's story was true: it was only through submitting to *the* Master, the Lord of the universe, that I was able to find the freedom I so desperately wanted.

Reflection

- How has your desire for freedom stolen freedoms from you?
- What authorities do you struggle to trust the most? Why?
- How do you view your occupational authority?
- How can you take ground in belonging to a church and being known there?

4
Work

"Congratulations! You're an adult. Now get to work."

Besides freedom, work is the other big thing that makes adulthood different from childhood. Sure, you might work some as a child, but your main role is to be a student. In fact, you're legally required to go to school as a child, while the law restricts how much a child can work. A kid's "job" is to learn and be trained so that they'll be capable of taking on a real job someday.

And now that day is here. You're responsible for yourself; your parents are no longer required or expected to take care of you. You have to pay for your own food, housing, transportation, insurance, and bills. Yay.

Many of you are actually excited by this fact, because now it means you can get your "dream job." You can do the thing you're so passionate about that you've spent years studying it and have invested many thousands of dollars (which you likely now owe as debt) to get a degree that will allow you at least a chance at getting the job. Now your life will finally be fun and fulfilling because you'll be spending your time doing what you've always wanted to do.

Yeah. I hate to burst your bubble, but it rarely ever works like that. If it did, you wouldn't see people constantly hopping from job to job to job. Today's young adults are famous for this, with Millennials changing jobs, on average, every two years.[1] That works out to something like two dozen different jobs over the course of a career. Baby Boomers, in comparison, stay at a job for an average of seven years. That means they'll have about six jobs in a lifetime. Go back one or two generations before that, and it seems most people had only one job in their entire lifetime. Clearly, something's changed, and it doesn't seem to be a change for the better.

Follow Your Passion

I've experienced this in my own life. In fact, I didn't make it two years in most of my early jobs.

When I was eighteen, my mom came to me and sat me down for a serious talk about my future. She's a school counselor, so she does this for a living. She asked me, "Where do you want to go to college?"

Now, you may have known the answer to this question since you were in the third grade, but what's crazy is that I hadn't thought about it much. So my answer was "I don't know."

She said, "Well, what do you want to study?"

"Nothing," I said, with complete honesty. I didn't like studying.

So then she asked this question: "What are you passionate about?"

I didn't have any kind of profound answer. Remember, I was just a confused high school kid at this point. What was I passionate about? I didn't know. Being liked? *Dawson's Creek*? Spring break? Beer? Skateboarding? Art?

"What did you just say?" my mom asked.

"Art?"

"We can work with that."

I asked what she had in mind, and she said there's this little school in Waco, Texas, where people can go and study art. That's cool, I said. Sounds great. I'll go and do that.

So I did. I moved to Waco and I went to this little technical school. I studied art. I was there for two years and graduated with a two-year degree. I got a diploma. I was ready to go to work.

But here's what I learned in college: I'm passionate about art when I can do it on my own terms and create whatever I want. I'm not passionate about art as an assignment. I don't like someone telling me what to create or having a say over what it should look like—which describes almost any art job I would be able to get. I had this diploma saying that I could do art for a living, but it was pretty much worthless, because I didn't want to do it for a living.

So I came back to the question: *What am I passionate about?* But I still didn't know. I was just a slightly older version of the eighteen-year-old me. I was passionate about a lot of the same things, except now instead of *Dawson's Creek* it was *One Tree Hill*. I was passionate about eating and not starving to death. So I needed to make money, which meant I needed a job.

I remember waking up early one morning in Waco and praying, "God, I need a job." I didn't even know where to look for a job, so I ended up going to the mall. It wasn't open yet. So I sat in the parking lot and prayed some more. "Lord, give me a job." When the mall opened, I went walking through it.

This girl came up to me in the mall and asked, "Hey, what do you do?" I told her that I was looking for a job.

She said, "You want to manage an Abercrombie & Fitch?"

"Yes, I do. So much."

She asked, "Where?"

I said, "How about Dallas?"

"Done."

I was like, *This is how this prayer thing works? This is amazing.*

You know those guys who stand in front of Abercrombie stores with their shirts off? I was not one of those guys. Instead, my job involved things like folding clothes. At midnight. I learned that I wasn't very passionate about that particular job. So, I thought, I needed to find a new job that I would be passionate about.

So I changed jobs and went to work at a gym. I figured I could get paid to work out. Now I was selling gym memberships, and I learned I wasn't passionate about that either.

So I changed jobs again and went to work for this design company, doing graphic design. I thought, *Great, now I can put my art degree to use!* But then I remembered that I wasn't passionate about doing other people's art.

So I changed jobs again and went to work for a telecommunications company, doing sales. I worked for more than one telecommunications company, actually, changing jobs a few more times. But I learned that I wasn't passionate about any of them.

So I changed jobs again. I went to work for an IT consulting firm, and I learned I wasn't passionate about that.

At about this time in my life, I realized that I was passionate about making money, and I was passionate about myself and my own happiness, but I wasn't passionate about or happy with any job I'd ever had. And I kind of found myself despairing a little bit. I had what some people call a "quarter-life crisis," and I wasn't even twenty-five yet.

I don't know if you've ever been there, but you can get really philosophical in these times. I'd have thoughts like, *What if I'm supposed to be a race car driver? What if I'm the fastest race car driver in the world, and I just don't know it, because I've never driven one? I need to find this out.* I'd have these kinds of discussions with my friends, usually while sitting on a tailgate with a beer in my hand. I would usually end up with something like, "I just want to live in a shack on the beach and surf." My buddies would point out the obvious: "Have you ever surfed?" "No, but I bet I could." Have you ever had one of these conversations? They are adulting at its best.

This was before I was following Christ, but there's a Christian version of this too. It's called "I think I need to move to Africa." You know: dig wells, feed the children, become a missionary. I don't know why, but for some reason, when Christians hit that wall, they all end up in Africa.

You would think, with all this introspection and thinking about what we truly want to do, we'd be really good at picking the right job or career field. But we're not. We're awful at it. We're the worst there's ever been, going through dozens of jobs to find the "right" one.

It's not your fault. You've been fed a lot of bad advice on this topic. There's this phrase we've all been taught: "Follow your passion." You might think that's always been the advice given to young people starting out in the world, but that's not actually the case. In fact, when looking at the trends of word usage in literature, the phrase "follow your passion" was virtually nonexistent in books before 1980. By 1990, though, it was showing up 1.5 million times. In the 2000s, the phrase skyrocketed; by 2008, it was being used over 21 million times in English literature. This isn't because of the rise of the internet; we're only talking about print books here. And it's not because there are suddenly more books; the percentage of books using the phrase has skyrocketed. If you look at other terms, like "career," or "job," or "love," the *percentage* of books using those words has remained relatively flat. It's the exact phrase "follow your passion" that has become popular in our lifetimes. "Follow your passion" is what you've been sold for the past twenty years.

The problem is, that's really, really bad advice.

It's bad advice because, well, we're talking about passions here. Passions are not logical. If everybody really followed their passions, society would quickly collapse. Nobody I know is passionate about picking up trash or cleaning clogged toilets or fixing roads or driving delivery trucks. None of those jobs would ever get done. Everyone would be too busy trying to launch their singing/modeling/acting/sports careers, with nobody left to form an audience.

Taken to its logical end, having everyone follow all their passions would lead to all kinds of sin and even to violent crime ("crimes of passion"). I know that's an extreme example, but it shows how following your passions is a really bad principle at its core.

It's also pretty much the opposite of what God's Word teaches. We're not supposed to follow our passions; we're supposed to bring our passions under control (Gal. 5:24). Instead of following our hearts (Jer. 17:9), we're called to follow God and become passionate about what he's passionate about.

Does that mean you should work at a job you're not passionate about? Maybe. It depends on the situation. If you have a job that you are passionate about, that's great. Work hard at it. Be a great employee. But if you can't find such a job, or you have a job you're not passionate about—well, you're still called to work (Prov. 14:23; 2 Thess. 3:10). So find a job you're not passionate about and work hard at that job. Be a great employee.

Let's face reality: you don't have to love your job. It's not a requirement. It's not necessary for success. You don't get paid for enjoying it. In fact, the very reason you get paid for working is because you're doing something that somebody else doesn't want to do, or simply can't do, and they're willing to pay money for someone else to do it. If it were enjoyable, you probably wouldn't get paid for it. It would be a hobby, not a job.

Plus, we're talking about your first real job (or one of your first). By definition, you're going to start out at the bottom of the ladder. Few people have a dream job that would be considered entry-level. I've heard employers complain that young adults today come into the workforce with unrealistic expectations; they think that they'll immediately be put to work doing something interesting and important.

They think they'll be granted power, authority, and respect within the company. That's not how the world works. You have to earn your employer's trust, which takes time and experience faithfully doing what they ask you to do—even if they ask you to just make coffee or collate papers at first. You also have to learn. School may teach you a lot of things, but it typically doesn't teach you the specifics of how to do a particular job for a particular company. After some time and some on-the-job training, then you might reach a place where you start getting to do more of what you really want to do.

Proverbs 22:29 says, "Do you see someone skilled in their work? They will serve before kings; they will not serve before officials of low rank." In other words, if you're really good at what you do, you'll be recognized for it and be given a more important position. What that proverb doesn't say, but definitely implies, is that it will take time before you're able to "serve before kings." It takes time, and a lot of faithful work and repetition, before you become truly skilled at anything. And it takes more time after that to be noticed for your work. If you want a surefire way to derail that, try hopping from job to job (like I did) trying to find one that will finally make you happy.

When it comes to work, my friend Jennie Allen put it brilliantly on her Facebook page:

A lot of my job is outside of my gifting and outside of my happy place. I'm a creative who created and now I have to do a lot of uncreative work to keep everything healthy and growing. I can hire and delegate and hand off and I have and I do and I will. HOWEVER, as a generation, we are desperate to find jobs we adore and are perfectly in our sweet spots. But it's not a realistic view of work. So whether it's mothering, medicine, CEO, sales, teaching, ministry, writing or so on . . . it is important to remember toil in work was a part of the curse and it is difficult and you do the things you don't like because it's RIGHT and OBEDIENT and HOLY. And on the days work is fun, smile and celebrate, and on the days work isn't fun, don't rethink your whole life. Do the work. And through it we are becoming more humble and holy.

Why We Work

If we want to be happy with our jobs, we need to change our perspective on why we work.

We don't work because it provides fulfillment or gives meaning to our lives or because we're passionate about it.

We work so that we'll have something to eat and something to wear and somewhere to live. We work to provide, both for ourselves and for others.

That's a lot different from how we usually look at work. We tend to treat our jobs as a core part—or even *the* core—of who we are. Think about when you meet someone for the first time. About 99 percent of the time, one of the first questions asked is "What do you do?" And 99 percent of the time, the answer is "I'm a (insert job title)." As if that's your identity, or the most important thing you do. It's like saying: "I'm not a dad or a husband or a great friend or a child of God on a mission to change the eternity of every person I meet. No, I'm a salesperson. My purpose in life is to sell things." There are many things about you that are, or should be, more important than your job title.

We work to provide. It's because, frankly, we need the money. If your job suddenly stopped paying you, I doubt you'd keep working there for long; you'd start looking for another job that pays money.

If that seems to make work sound a lot less romantic, well, good. Your job's not supposed to be your idol. It was never meant to fulfill you. It's a necessary thing, and a good thing, but it's not the ultimate thing. It's a means to provide.

Who, or what, are we supposed to provide for?

First Timothy 5:8 says that we are to provide for our families. In fact, it says that "Anyone who does not provide for their relatives, and especially for their own household, has denied the faith and is worse than an unbeliever." That may sound pretty harsh, but it's harsh for a reason: because it's really, really important. If you are able to work and capable of providing, then God commands you to do so.

Providing for your "household" might sound kind of funny as a single adult, when you're the head of a household of one. But remember that it also means you'll have to provide for your *future* family. Want to be married and have kids someday? That means you'll have these things the IRS calls "dependents," and they'll be fully dependent on you to provide for them. Work hard now and be wise with the money you earn, and you'll build good habits and a good foundation for your future family.

We're also called to provide for those in need who are unable to provide for themselves. First John 3:17 says that "If anyone has material possessions and sees a brother or sister in need but has no pity on them, how can the love of God be in that person?" And Matthew 25:31–46 says that helping the needy counts as helping God himself.

And then there's probably the most important part, from an eternal perspective: we're to work so we can provide for the mission of advancing the gospel. The apostle Paul gave an example of that. Though you probably think of him as a missionary and a full-time evangelist, Paul actually worked as a tentmaker (Acts 18:2–4). He made tents to support himself and his traveling companions so that they could afford to spread the gospel (Acts 20:33–35; 2 Thess. 3:7–9). His job supported his mission.

Was Paul passionate about building tents? I don't know. I doubt it, though, because he didn't talk about it much in all his writings. My guess is that he made tents because he needed to provide, and being a tentmaker was a good way to do that. It's a job he could do anywhere, as he traveled from city to city sharing the gospel. And it would have flexible hours; he could work at any time of the day or night, which allowed him to preach and minister to people whenever the opportunity presented itself. He was passionate about spreading the gospel, and making tents was a means to that end.

Work as Worship

Even though Paul might not have been passionate about making tents, I'd bet that he did an excellent job. His tents were probably the best you could buy. This is the guy who wrote, in Colossians 3:23–24, "Whatever you do, work at it with all your heart, as working for the Lord, not for human masters, since you know that you will receive an inheritance from the Lord as a reward. It is the Lord Christ you are serving." He saw his job as working for the Lord, the One he was so passionate about serving and spreading the good news about.

You don't have to love your job to be good at it or to work hard at it. We're *commanded* to work hard, regardless of whether we like the job or feel passionate about it. When we do so, especially if it's for a job or a boss we don't like, we earn more than just a paycheck. We'll receive an eternal reward for serving Christ through the way we work.

How you work will also have an impact on those you work with. Philippians 2:14–16 says that we are to "Do everything without grumbling or arguing, so that you may become blameless and pure, 'children of God without fault in a warped and crooked generation.' Then you will shine among them like stars in the sky as you hold firmly to the word of life." How we work, and the way we honor our employers by doing our best for them, is supposed to stand out as different from the rest of the world. It's supposed to make people notice and make them more willing to listen to us when we explain why we work that way. We're to be "the light of the world" and "let [our] light shine before others" (Matt. 5:14–16), and that includes shining at work.

I've been on a number of what some people call "mission trips." I've traveled to Haiti to share the gospel there. I've traveled to the heart of Africa, to places so far away and so remote that it takes several planes and two full days of flying to get there. I've traveled to villages in the Amazon rain forest that can only be reached by boat. Each time, it took a lot of planning, a lot of time away from family, and quite a bit of money to make the trip. And it was totally worth it, because sharing the gospel is that important. It allowed me to be a light to the world.

However, even having been to all those places, the darkest mission field I've ever seen is corporate America. It's the place where your light can shine the brightest. Our workplaces need the gospel just as much as any village in the jungle. And here's the deal: you can pay thousands of dollars to go on a "mission trip" overseas for a week, or you can *get paid* to go to work every day and be on mission there. They literally pay you to be there! And you don't need a translator; you speak the language. You don't need to study and learn about a new culture; it's your culture. From a mission perspective, it almost seems too good to be true.

I'm reminded of the story of Mark Whitacre. You probably haven't heard of him, but you probably have heard of Matt Damon, who played Mark Whitacre in a movie based on his life, *The Informant!* Mark worked for Archer Daniels Midland, or ADM, a food processing company. Probably doesn't sound like the most exciting career field, right? However, Mark knew about some shady dealings going on at ADM, involving the largest price-fixing scandal in American history. He contacted the FBI, and the FBI asked him to serve as an undercover agent, secretly recording conversations and gathering evidence to build a criminal case against ADM executives.

So imagine yourself in Mark's shoes: one day he's working his desk job in the exciting world of food processing, and the next day he's an undercover spy for the FBI. That probably made his workdays a bit more exciting, don't you think? His job didn't change; he still did the same work as before. But now he was on a mission for a higher authority. He was on mission, at his job. And that's what you can be: on mission—for God, not the FBI—at your job. You can do your work while working for a higher purpose.

You Are Made to Work

It's true that work can be a pain at times. That's a result of the fall; because of sin, nothing in this world is perfect. It's because of our fallen world that Genesis 3:17 talks about "painful toil":

> Cursed is the ground because of you;
> through painful toil you will eat food from it
> all the days of your life.

However, though the pain of work is a consequence of the fall, work itself is not a punishment. In a perfect world, we would still work. How do I know this? Because before the fall, in the Garden of Eden when it was a perfect world, humankind was still commanded to work. Genesis 2:15 says that "The LORD God took the man and put him in the Garden of Eden to work it and take care of it." This was before sin entered the picture, and before the curse of Genesis 3:17.

And in heaven, where everything will again be perfect, we'll still have work to do. In the very last chapter of the Bible, Revelation 22:3 says, "No longer will there be any curse. The throne of God and of the Lamb will be in the city, and his servants will serve him." We'll work serving God, but work will no longer be cursed.

In other words, we're created to work. It's something we're made to do, and it's not punishment in and of itself. Paradise is not eternally sitting on a beach, couch, or cloud with nothing to do. That gets boring really fast. Paradise is working the way God intended and joyfully serving him through that work. When we joyfully serve him through our work today we are showing the world a preview of paradise by being a reflection of God and his coming kingdom.

> Whatever you do, work at it with all your heart, as working for the Lord, not for human masters, since you know that you will receive an inheritance from the Lord as a reward. It is the Lord Christ you are serving. (Col. 3:23–24)

"Whatever you do"—which covers everything you do and every possible job—work hard at it. Serve God through it. And you might find that you start to actually like it.

Reflection

- Why do you work?
- Do you truly work as though you are "working for the Lord" (Col. 3:23)? How would your attitude at work change if you were?
- Are you too focused on your job? Are you not focused enough?

5
Money

IT'S NOT ALL ABOUT THE BENJAMINS

My first job after college—the one I got in the mall at Abercrombie & Fitch—paid $23,000 a year. Before that, I was used to making more like $5,000 a year working part-time, so $23,000 seemed like a lot of money. When I first heard how much I'd be earning at my new job, I felt rich. I thought, *What am I going to do with all this money? There's no way I could spend that much.*

That $23,000 was more than enough. At first. But soon I started noticing some nicer things I wanted to buy but couldn't afford. I met people with other jobs that clearly paid more than my job did. I went from feeling ecstatic about my paycheck to being discontented. It was no longer enough.

So I went out and found one of those other jobs that did pay more. I was glad to be making more money—but not as happy or excited as when I first got the call saying I would be making $23,000 a year. It still wasn't enough. So I sought to make more money. And more. I got to where I was making twice as much as when I started. It wasn't enough. Three times as much: not enough. Five times as much: not enough. Even when I found myself in a business development job making ten times as much, it still was not enough. I was never happy with what I had. I wanted more.

The Money Myth

Jesus talked about money more than any other topic. You might think that an eternal God would be too big and too holy to talk about something as seemingly petty and unimportant as money. But he does talk about it, a lot, and for good reason: money causes more problems for more people than just about anything else in this life.

Technically, money itself—or even the lack of it—isn't the issue for most people. Money isn't a problem by itself. It's the way we relate to it, including the efforts we take to earn it and the ways we choose to manage it, that causes problems. It can steal your joy, put you in bondage, or cause you to waste your life in pursuit of the wrong thing.

The reason that money causes so many problems is because of a persistent myth, one that almost every person (myself included) tends to believe. The myth is this: having more money will make you happy.

Note the "more" in that sentence. That's one of the key problems with this idea: it's always about having "more" money. It's not about having "enough" money. It's not even about having "a lot" of money. It's about having *more* money than you currently do. Regardless of how much money they currently have, almost everyone thinks that if they just had *more* money, they'd finally be happy.

But there's no end to that. That's a destination that never comes. There's never a level you can reach where it's no longer possible to make more money. The myth that more money will make you happy will have you always striving to collect more, no matter how much you already have. Trust me; I've lived it out. I've tested the idea personally. And if you think that somehow I just didn't reach a high enough level of income before giving up, look at the billionaires in our world. A billion is a thousand millions, which means they could buy at least a thousand million-dollar items—or live off a million dollars a year for a *thousand years*. Logically, there's nothing really to be gained by a billionaire making more money. It won't change anything for them. So do billionaires still try to make more money? Absolutely. They're more focused on increasing their wealth than just about anyone else I've ever seen. Warren Buffett, currently the third wealthiest person in the world, is still working at the age of eighty-seven. He could have retired decades ago and lived the rest of his life like a king (literally), yet he's still out there trying to make more money.

Speaking of kings, one of the richest men to have ever lived is King Solomon. His annual income was measured not in thousands of dollars but in how many thousands of pounds of gold he took home per year. (About fifty thousand pounds, by the way, which at today's prices is just shy of a billion dollars. Per year. He didn't have a net worth of a billion dollars; he had a tax-free annual income of a billion dollars, or about three million per day.)[1] So was he a happy guy? Well, go read Ecclesiastes, which he wrote. Solomon's first words in Ecclesiastes are: "Meaningless! Meaningless! . . . Utterly meaningless! Everything is meaningless" (Eccles. 1:2). And then it kind of goes downhill from there. Clearly, having more money didn't make Solomon all that happy. (Really, go read Ecclesiastes. It's a fascinating perspective from someone who literally had everything you could ever want.)

There's even scientific evidence that having more money doesn't make you happier. For instance, researchers have published a study that looked at how happiness relates to income.[2] They found that once you reached a certain income level, making more money beyond that level did not make you any happier. What's interesting is that the dollar amount wasn't crazy high, like a million dollars; it was only about $75,000. I'm not saying that's a small amount, but think of what that means: someone who makes a million dollars a year is, on average, no happier than a family that is right in the middle of the middle class. That last $925,000 does *nothing* to increase their happiness. They could give it all up and still be just as happy.

If all the evidence shows that making more money doesn't make anyone happier, then why does almost everyone believe it does?

The Comparison Game

The biggest problem, in my opinion, is that we all play the comparison game. We compare ourselves to others, and we want to have at least as much money, or preferably more, than they have.

It's a weird competition that there's no prize for winning. We're fairly happy until we see someone who appears to have more than we do, and then we suddenly don't feel like we have enough.

It also means that our satisfaction is dependent on our surroundings. I've been to countries where the economic landscape is quite different than what we have in the United States. Places like Haiti, where the average annual income is about $350, or less than one dollar per day. Now, if money made you happy, then Haiti would have some of the saddest people on earth. But that's not the case at all. People there were just as happy, or maybe even happier, than the average person in the US making two hundred times as much money. The difference? They're not looking at their neighbor living in a five-bedroom house and driving a Mercedes and thinking, *If I just had that, I'd be happy.* If they were comparing their situation to that, they wouldn't be very content. But their neighbors don't have any of that stuff. No, they're looking at their neighbor living in a one-room shack, and even if it's a slightly nicer shack than theirs, it's probably not something that would create a lot of envy.

I've heard it said that comparison is the thief of all joy, and that's definitely been the case in my own life. I'm happy with what I have until I see somebody who has more. And then, though my own situation has not changed at all, I'm suddenly no longer happy with what I have. It has played out over and over again in my past. Sadly, what you have doesn't have much to do with your unhappiness; it's what you notice that others have, which you then want.

But it doesn't have to be that way. If you have the right view of money, you can keep it from ruling over you.

Self-Worth vs. Net Worth

To have the right view of money, it's important to understand what money is not.

For starters, money is not a measure of how much you are worth. You are priceless, meaning you have a value that can't even be measured by a price. A person's life is not worth more because they have a million dollars, and their life is not worth less if they have zero dollars. The same person can go from being broke to having a million dollars, and then lose everything and be broke again, and their actual value as a human being doesn't change at all.

It can be confusing because of how our society talks about money. We use terminology like "net worth," or talk about someone being worth X amount of money. But that's not how much you are worth; that's how much *the things in your possession* are worth. If you sold off everything you owned and paid off all your debts, however much money is left would be your net worth. You're not a better person or more valuable to God and to the people who love you if your net worth goes up. And if you were to willingly give it all away, that wouldn't make you a worthless person because your net worth would then be zero. If anything, using money in that way to help others in need makes you a more valuable person.

Money Is Not Success

Similarly, money does not equal success.

People often use the word *success* as a stand-in for *money*. If you say that someone is "successful," what you usually mean is that they make a lot of money.

But really, *success* simply means that you have accomplished whatever you set out to do. For some people, making money is their main goal in life, so getting a raise or taking on a higher-paying job does mean that they've been successful at that particular goal. But that's really not a very exciting goal, when you think about it. How about the goal of raising godly children who will be equipped to make wise choices throughout their lives? That's a big goal my wife is working toward all day, every day. Though she doesn't make any money at all doing it, being successful at that job will have a far greater impact than somebody who ignores their children in pursuit of making even more money. Or what about being successful at sharing the gospel? That affects someone for eternity, which means it's a far bigger success than merely having a million dollars to spend on temporary pleasures.

You can be really successful at collecting green-tinged portraits of dead presidents or you can be really successful at something that truly matters. But it's hard to do both.

Money Does Not Equal Security

One of the reasons people chase after money is because they are seeking security. They don't want to worry about whether they'll have enough money to afford their vacations or to send their kids to private school or to pay the bills if they get laid off. The big one, of course, is saving for retirement and storing up enough money so that you never have to work again for the rest of your life.

This might seem like a good idea. After all, it is wise to be prepared for contingencies. The book of Proverbs talks about storing up for a future season like an ant stores up food for the winter. As with so many good things, though, saving money becomes a problem when taken to extremes or done for the wrong reasons. It can rapidly become an idol, causing us to trust in our money for security rather than trusting in

God. In the United States, every dollar bill has "In God We Trust" written on it for a reason.

Jesus spoke very bluntly on this subject. In Matthew 6:25–34, he tells us not to waste our lives worrying about whether we'll have enough to live on. "Look at the birds of the air; they do not sow or reap or store away in barns, and yet your heavenly Father feeds them. Are you not much more valuable than they? Can any one of you by worrying add a single hour to your life?" (vv. 26–27). The answer to that question, by the way, is a resounding no; stress and worrying have been shown to actually reduce people's life spans.

Then you have the parable of the rich fool: someone who had worked hard to store up enough resources so he could essentially retire early. As Jesus tells the story in Luke 12:18–20, "Then he said, 'This is what I'll do. I will tear down my barns and build bigger ones, and there I will store my surplus grain. And I'll say to myself, "You have plenty of grain laid up for many years. Take life easy; eat, drink and be merry."' But God said to him, 'You fool! This very night your life will be demanded from you. Then who will get what you have prepared for yourself?'"

In other words, you have no idea what is going to happen. You may save up for retirement and never even make it that far. Money's not going to buy you long life, and you can't take it with you when you go.

Even money itself is not trustworthy; it's just paper, and only has value because people treat it as if it has value. People in many countries have learned this lesson the hard way, as money suddenly became less valuable. I own an authentic one-hundred-billion-dollar bill ($100,000,000,000) from Zimbabwe that I bought on eBay for just a few American dollars to remind me of this. There have been many examples over just the past few decades of countries where money became worthless, and it took bags or shopping carts full of cash just to buy a loaf of bread.[3] People's entire life savings—even for rich people—were suddenly worth less than the cost of their next meal. Look up "hyperinflation," if you're curious about just how bad it can get.

And don't think we're immune to it in the United States. Money disappears here with some regularity. During the last major downturn, in 2008, an estimated $14 trillion in household wealth evaporated. That is more than $40,000 per person. That's money people thought they had saved up, and suddenly it no longer existed. The value of it just vanished.

The point is simply this: don't put your trust in money. It's not trustworthy.

Money Is Not Evil

At this point, you may be thinking, *I get it. Money is bad. As the saying goes, "Money is the root of all evil."*

In case you're wondering, that old saying does come from the Bible. However, it's a misquote. Almost every time I've heard it, it's been quoted like that: "Money is the root of all evil." However, the actual quote, from 1 Timothy 6:10, is "The love of money is a root of all kinds of evil." That's an essential distinction: it's the love of money, and not money itself, that is a problem. (It's also just a root of all kinds of evil, not *the* root of all evil.)

Money itself is not evil. It's neither good nor bad. It's morally neutral. It can be used for either good or evil; the same money could be used to either feed a hungry child or feed an unhealthy addiction. But that's based on what you do with it, not the nature of the money itself.

And that's why the *love* of money is a root of all kinds of evil: it affects what you do with money and what you are willing to do to get money. As the preceding verse says, "Those who want to get rich fall into temptation and a trap and into many foolish and harmful desires that plunge people into ruin and destruction" (v. 9).

The love of money can cause you to behave unethically. To take advantage of people. To take risks that are unwise. Or it can simply make you spend your life working really hard in order to store up treasure that will not last and will not make you happy, while neglecting the things that are really important.

If money itself was evil, the answer would be simple: just get rid of it. All of it. Don't have any money. Most people, I've found, aren't that interested in doing that. And since you do have money—and probably quite a bit of it, since even the poverty level in the US is ridiculously rich by the standards of most of the world—you're faced with a more challenging task: how to use that money wisely and keep it from becoming a problem.

What Money Is

Besides looking at all the things that money is not, perhaps we should also look at what it is.

Money is a tool. It is something that can be used to do work and to accomplish something. For example, it can be used to pay your bills, providing you with a place to live and food to eat. It can also be used to help others, providing them with a place to live and food to eat. As with any tool, it can be used for something good or something bad.

Because of this, money is also a responsibility. It's a tool you have that gives you the power to do either good or evil, and you have to decide what to do with it. You choose how to steward it and where to spend or invest it. You're responsible for what that money does.

Understanding this next reality will help you tremendously in your view of money: you have no money. All money is ultimately God's money. As with every resource on this earth, God created it and gave it to us to steward during our lifetimes. Now, that's definitely *not* the attitude most people take toward money. People tend to see it as *their* money, something they have earned on their own and therefore something they can choose to use as they wish. "Nobody gave it to me," you might argue. "I worked for it and earned it on my own."

I'm not saying you haven't worked for whatever money you have. And in that sense, you did earn it. But my question would be: Who gave you the ability to work? How come you are able to earn that money?

Again, many people would point to their own accomplishments: you are able to do a certain job because you worked hard to get an education, or to gain the experience and necessary skills—skills that are worth paying for. OK, so: What made you able to learn those skills? You worked hard—what made you able to work at all? It's great that you applied yourself, but that means you had something to apply. Who made you, gave you gifts, allowed you to be born where you were, live where you do, and find the opportunities that you've found?

Locally, there is a much-beloved NBA player named Dirk Nowitzki. He's played with the Dallas Mavericks for twenty years and is considered one of the greatest power forwards to ever play the game. He's especially known for being a great shooter, a skill he's doubtlessly practiced millions of times. In other words, Dirk Nowitzki has worked very hard to be a great basketball player.

However, Dirk is also literally seven feet tall. There are very few people who can list their height on their driver's license as 7'0". Now, being 7'0" doesn't automatically make you a great basketball player. I'm pretty tall myself, at 6'7", and I never had a shot at the NBA. Dirk is great at basketball both because he is super tall *and* because he has worked super hard at it. However, he did absolutely nothing to earn the "tall" part. And without being tall, no matter how hard he worked or how much he practiced, he never would have become a great NBA power forward. There are no great 5'4" NBA power forwards and there never will be.

Basically, it comes down to: What did you do to earn having a brain? What work did you do to learn how to have hands and fingers attached to your arms? That air you're breathing: What did you do to earn that? Everything you have, every ability you have, and every second of life you have is a gift from God. And that means every cent you have, no matter how hard you worked for it, is only in your pocket because of God's gifts.

Jesus talked specifically about this in the parable of the talents, which you can find in Matthew 25:14–30. It's the story of a master (representing God) who entrusts his wealth to his servants (representing us) for a time. The money was measured in talents, which is a weight of gold. In teaching on this passage, people often talk about God giving us "talents," such as natural abilities or skills. And he does, absolutely, give us those talents. But we can't ignore the fact that Jesus was literally talking about money here. He was saying that money is *not* ours but is merely a resource that God has given us to steward for him. And the parable emphasizes that we are to do something worthwhile with that money.

You could say that money is a test. It's not a test as in something that God puts before us to trip us up, or a way for him to find out something about our character (as if he didn't already know). But it is a litmus test for ourselves that shows us the condition of our heart. Jesus said:

> Whoever can be trusted with very little can also be trusted with much, and whoever is dishonest with very little will also be dishonest with much. So if you have not been trustworthy in handling worldly wealth, who will trust you with true riches? And if you have not been trustworthy with someone else's property, who will give you property of your own?
>
> No one can serve two masters. Either you will hate the one and love the other, or you will be devoted to the one and despise the other. You cannot serve both God and money. (Luke 16:10–13)

Don't make the mistake of thinking Jesus is just talking about eternal riches. I fully acknowledge that lots of wicked people have lots of money. The Bible is clear, however, that you are to steward the money God has entrusted to you to the very best of your ability. It's his money. Once, to illustrate this point, we gave out money during a sermon at The Porch. That's right: people came to church and instead of giving money they received it. Instead of passing around an offering plate, we passed around envelopes full of money. Some received a few dollars, some received a twenty-dollar bill, and some got one hundred dollars or more. People were excited to get money. Then, however, we asked them to use that money to do something good. There were two stipulations: they couldn't simply give it back to the church, and they had to let us know what good thing they did with it. Suddenly, people saw this "gift" as a responsibility. Some people even saw it as a burden. This is the reality for a steward. We steward God's resources for him. It is his money that we have on loan.

Again, the question becomes whether you love money. Is it a tool, or is it your treasure?

Principles for Handling Money

So what should you do with the money you're given in the time you're here on earth? Based on God's wisdom, lessons I've learned, and things I've observed, here are some principles to keep in mind when making decisions about money.

Live below Your Means

In other words, spend less money than you make. If you make a lot of money, live as if you don't; the extra money you save can be used to do a lot of good for those who have less. If you don't make much money, this may mean that you have to live very frugally. That's fine; if you have the necessities, you won't be missing out on anything important. As long as you avoid playing the comparison game, it won't make you any less happy. Besides, it's really the only option you have long-term; you can't continually spend more than you earn without piling up insurmountable debt. Some people try to bet on the future, living beyond their means now in the hope that their income will catch up to their lifestyle. That's a big mistake; you have no idea what is going to happen tomorrow

(James 4:13–16). It's also a mistake because of how interest works: money saved now is worth more than money saved later, while every dollar of debt you accumulate now can cost you several dollars to pay off in the future.

Be Wary of Debt

Limit your debt. Work to pay off debt you have and be very careful about taking on new debt. I won't say to avoid debt completely, because God doesn't forbid debt, and good arguments can be made in favor of some kinds of debt. A home mortgage is debt, for instance, and in some cases (certainly not all) buying a home can make more financial sense than renting. Student loans can potentially be wise if the degree you get allows you to land a job that pays enough to cover the cost of the loans. (This is not always the case, so student loans are sometimes a bad idea.) Businesses may require loans in order to make money, which can then be used to pay back the loans. Far too often, though, debt becomes a trap that can hold you in financial bondage. "The rich rule over the poor, and the borrower is slave to the lender" (Prov. 22:7).

Avoid Credit Card Debt Like the Plague

Even in cases where having debt might make sense, putting that debt on a credit card does not make sense. Credit cards charge ridiculously high interest, and their "minimum payment" structure encourages you to keep paying that high interest for years and years. The smart way to use a credit card is to pay off the balance in full every month and to make sure it doesn't tempt you to spend money you don't have. If it becomes a problem, stick to debit cards or cash instead.

Have a Budget

You really need to know how much money you're making, how much you're spending, and what you're spending it on. Otherwise, you can't evaluate how well you're stewarding your money, and you'll have no guidelines for how much you should be spending on different things. It might seem like a pain, but there are free tools online these days that make it fairly easy. (Mint seems to be the most popular free budgeting app, and the basic version of EveryDollar is also free. Mvelope and YNAB [short for "You Need A Budget"] are other apps worth mentioning, though they may charge a small fee. There are other options, and I'm sure they all work just fine; the key is to actually use one.)

Buy Less Stuff

What you're really looking for is happiness, and stuff doesn't make you happy. I should know; I'm one of those guys who tried buying a lot of stuff. A nicer car or a nice watch might have made me excited at first, but then it just became my old car or my old watch. And the more stuff you have, the more it has you. It will break down or require upgrades or get lost or stolen or make you nervous about the fact that it might get lost or stolen. Some stuff you may truly need, but a lot of stuff people buy these days is unnecessary.

Buy Experiences, Not Stuff

Studies have shown that buying experiences—for example, a backpacking trip through Europe, whitewater rafting with friends, or a live performance of your favorite band—provides more enjoyment than buying physical items.[4] Twenty years from now, the memories of that weekend road trip with your roommates will be worth far more to you than a twenty-year-old TV that has long since broken down and been thrown in the trash. Of course, you can also go too far with buying experiences, and you have to make sure they fit in your budget. But if you're looking for something fun, don't look for it in a store.

Be Generous

When God tells us to do something (or not do something), it is for our own good. Being generous is no exception. Again, science backs it up, showing that people are happier when they give to somebody else versus spending that money on themselves.[5] One study looked at 230,000 people around the world and found that people everywhere were happier when they were more generous, regardless of whether they were rich or were barely scraping by. Want to be happy? Be a cheerful giver (2 Cor. 9:7). Give often and be creative in doing so. I'm not sure how God will call you to give, but be ready for it.

Don't Put Your Trust in Money

For reasons I've already talked about, don't put your trust in money. Trust in God, who has promised to provide everything you really need. For some of us this will require quite the undoing. It will start with an honest evaluation of "What do I trust in?"

Don't Waste Your Life Chasing after Money

It's so common that it's become a cliché. Think of how many movies or shows or books feature a character—often a father—who is so focused on making money that he neglects his children, shuns his spouse (or love interest), misses out on fun experiences, and ignores or even mistreats people in need. Don't be that guy. Don't be a cliché.

Store Up Treasures in Heaven

Do not store up for yourselves treasures on earth, where moths and vermin destroy, and where thieves break in and steal. But store up for yourselves treasures in heaven, where moths and vermin do not destroy, and where thieves do not break in and steal. For where your treasure is, there your heart will be also. (Matt. 6:19–21)

You can invest in something temporary that is ultimately a depreciating asset. Or you can invest in something that you can enjoy forever and ever.

When talking about finances and investing, you may hear about the net present value of money, or NPV. Basically, NPV looks at the value you'll get from an investment over the coming years and calculates how much that future value is worth to you in today's dollars. That's why people buy investments: they figure that the future income they'll receive from the investment, which may be spread out over many years, is worth more than what it costs them today.

A funny thing happens when you apply that investment logic to storing up treasures in heaven. Since treasures in heaven last forever, the value they provide continues for an infinite number of years. The net present value for even a single dollar's worth of treasure, calculated over an infinite number of future years, equals infinity. Its value to you right now is an infinite number of dollars. It's the best possible return on investment. So even if you were to store up billions of dollars in earthly treasure, its value today would be worth almost *nothing* compared to the value of the smallest possible treasure in heaven.

There's your investment strategy. Be generous with your time, treasure, and talents now, and you'll be paid back infinitely more throughout eternity.

Things Money Cannot Buy

Money can buy you many things that you *need*, which is a good thing. Food, clothing, shelter—you need those things. However, it can't buy anything that you really *want*. Money can't buy you happiness. It can't buy you love. It can't buy you friendship; any "friends" that are attracted to you because you have money are just taking advantage of you. And money can't buy you eternal life. It can't even add one hour to your life.

So be smart in how you deal with money. Use it for good. Control it so that it doesn't end up controlling you. Above all, don't let it have your heart. It's not worthy of your love.

Reflection

- Do you struggle most in the area of spending, saving, or generosity?
- How can you grow in viewing all of your resources as God's?
- How much more do you have than you need?
- What are the financial needs around you that you could meet?
- If someone was observing your life, would they say you trust in money or God?

Adulting
with
Friends

6
Community

YOUR PLAYMATES AND PLAYGROUNDS

When I was in middle school, I spent a lot of my time hanging out with a small group of friends. Though I lived in the country outside of town, the other four boys in our group all lived near each other in the same neighborhood. We were a real "band of brothers"; five boys who would spend our free time together, get into mischief together, and always have each other's backs. We spent the summers, weekends, and after-school hours together.

We definitely did things we shouldn't have done. Like most middle-schoolers, we weren't trying to follow Christ at the time, and we pretty much personified the definition of immaturity. For example, if one of us liked a girl, we would show our affection for her by TPing her house, wrapping it in toilet paper. We called our group the "Pearly Whites," because—again, the picture of immaturity—if someone drove by while we were TPing a house, we would turn around, drop our pants, and "moon" them.

Fast-forward to college, and I again had a band of brothers I would hang out with. It was a different town, different group of people, different stage of life, and different kinds of trouble we would get into, but the idea was still the same. We did life together. We had each other's backs. Once a guy picked a fight with me, and before I could get a punch off, he had been attacked by four of my closest friends. If one of us got in trouble, we were all thinking about how to get him out. We were as close as family—closer, actually, than I was with my family at that time—and we never had to be alone because we were always there for each other.

All of us have a deep desire within us for that kind of community, even from an early age. In kindergarten, we designate someone as a "best friend." We join teams or clubs at least partly so we can build relationships. We form groups of friends or cliques (or secretly wish we were part of one). We want to belong and be in close relationship with someone. It's a desire that's hard-wired into us.

As we become adults and are officially "independent," some people think that we no longer need close friends. This is a mistake. You don't grow out of your need for community. In fact, I'd argue it becomes even more important as you enter adulthood.

Not Good to Be Alone

Life is really all about relationships. It's not about work, or money, or material goods. You can be happy without those things, as long as you have healthy relationships. But it's much harder, if not impossible, to be happy if your relationships are broken (or nonexistent).

Most people are probably familiar with the Bible verse that says "It is not good for the man to be alone" (Gen. 2:18). If nothing else, you've probably heard it at a wedding. It's usually brought up in the context of marriage; after all, right after God made this observation, he created a woman (Eve) so that the man (Adam) wouldn't be alone.

This verse is talking about more than just marriage. After all, God didn't say "It is not good for the man to be single." He said it's not good for the man to be alone. It's not good for any man, or any member of humankind, to be alone. We were created to be in relationship with other people.

God's "not good" proclamation becomes more significant when you look at it in context. In Genesis 1, God has just created the universe and everything in it. He created everything in six days, and six times he declares that what he created was "good." He created light, and "saw that the light was good" (1:4). He created land and water, and "saw that it was good" (v. 10). He created plants, and "saw that it was good" (v. 12). And so on, six different times. After the sixth time of seeing that something was "good," he looked at everything all together and saw that it was "very good" (v. 31).

So, God has said over and over that all he has made was good, and then, for the very first time, he said that something was *not* good. This exception is kind of jarring. If something is not good, it's bad. Everything's been good, but now there was something wrong with creation. What's wrong? The man was alone. He's not supposed to be alone. That's not what God intended. So God solved the problem by creating another person for Adam to be in relationship with. In creating this one relationship, God created a way for humanity to multiply, offering the possibility of other relationships.

If you're going through this life alone—not "single," but "alone"—then that's bad. It goes against your very nature. It's not good to be alone.

Solitary Confinement

There's an extreme example from today's world that proves the point.

Society punishes those who break its laws by putting some of the worst offenders in prison. Part of the reason why prison is considered punishment is because it limits your access to family and friends. It makes you more alone, even if you are in a building with hundreds of other residents.

But what happens if someone who's already incarcerated breaks the rules of the prison? There's another level of punishment for such people, one that's considered much worse than merely being in prison. It's called solitary confinement. The person stays in the prison, they're still locked up, and the length of their sentence isn't changed; the only change is that they must spend the time alone. Other than the death penalty, that's the worst punishment our society has come up with: simply forcing you to be all alone. No human interaction whatsoever. And it's a terribly harsh punishment. But the reason why it's considered the strictest of punishments is because we are not meant to be alone. It goes against our very nature. We're created for close relationships.

The Lonely Generation

While solitary confinement is terrible, some free people willingly choose to isolate themselves. They're not confined, and they may physically be around a bunch of other people, but they choose to keep their distance relationally.

Today's young adults are literally the most "connected" generation in the history of the world. But they're also among the loneliest, with many of them having no close relationships of any kind. I call them "the lonely generation."

The statistics back this up. According to a study conducted by Duke University and the University of Arizona:

- Between 1985 and 2004, the number of people saying there was no one with whom they discussed important matters nearly tripled.
- 24.6 percent of Americans reported that they had no confidants, even counting close family members.
- Another 19.6 percent said they had just one confidant.
- More than half, 53.4 percent, did not have any confidants outside their family.[1]

Multiple other studies have shown that the loneliest people in society are young adults.[2] For example, one Australian study found that people ages 24–34 were by far the most likely to be lonely, with 30 percent saying they "frequently feel lonely." For comparison, among those ages 35–39, only 6 percent said they often felt lonely.[3]

Why is this? Better yet, how is this even possible?

It's not like this generation is composed of a lot of shepherds or hermits out in the wilderness who rarely see another human. We're more urban than ever; odds are, there are a few thousand people within a mile of where you live. We live in giant cities, in busy apartment complexes, and work in office cubicles where the walls between us are only four feet tall. Forget lonely; it seems like we'd have to work really hard to even be alone.

And that's not even accounting for technology, which allows us to talk with people and stay in relationship with them even if they're far away. Take Facebook, for example: the average adult Facebook user has 338 "friends" on the social network, and young adults tend to have even more than that.[4] And it's not like our generation is on just one social network; we also have Snapchat, Instagram, Twitter, LinkedIn, and a host of others. With so many friends and the ability to connect with them in so many ways, how could we possibly be lonely?

However, our extreme connectedness is part of the reason why we lack true connections. You can't have 338 close friends. It's impossible. There aren't enough hours in the day. You can have 338 acquaintances, or 338 people whom you've met and had a few conversations with. But how many people do you hang out with and discuss important life issues with on a daily or weekly basis? You might have 338 people in your phone's contact list, but how many of them have called you today just to see how you are doing?

This is why some people who seem to be the most outgoing, who know everyone and are always the life of the party, are still secretly lonely. Everyone knows who they are, but nobody really *knows* them. Nobody knows what's going on in their life, what they struggle with, or what dreams they want to fulfill. Casting a wide net and having hundreds of "friends" can actually be a way to intentionally avoid being known for who you are. On the flip side, just because someone is introverted or shy doesn't mean they have to be lonely. Such people can sometimes be better at developing deep relationships with a smaller number of friends.

Friends vs. Community

The message here is not just to have friends. It's to have people in your life who provide you with what I like to call *community*.

What do I mean by that?

A community is a group of people who are committed to being a part of your life and seeking what's best for you, no matter what. They care enough for you to speak the truth to you, even if the truth is hard to hear, and love you enough to provide tough love if needed.

Most "friends" don't fully fit that definition, and someone can be a part of your community even if they might not otherwise be someone you'd choose as a friend. Friendships are often based on common interests and proximity: a person you work with likes the same obscure British TV shows as you do, so you discuss the latest episodes and maybe hang out to watch them together. Or you meet someone on your softball team who also likes to compete in triathlons, and since you're both crazy that way, you start training together. Those friendships are fine, and they could develop into community, but they usually don't. And sometimes, if you move or your interests change, those friendships fall by the wayside.

Someone you're in community with might not share any of those surface-level common interests. They might, but it's not a prerequisite. But you will share one thing in common: an interest in doing what's best for each other and helping each other navigate the choices and decisions in life.

I've heard it said that a friend is someone who will come bail you out of jail, while a best friend is someone who is sitting beside you in that cell saying "Man, we really messed up this time." If that's the illustration, then community would be a group of people who did everything they could to keep you out of jail by addressing the pattern of bad decisions or the bad habits that they knew might land you there eventually. If you still ended up in jail, they'd come visit you there and bail you out if needed. But they also might intentionally *not* bail you out if, based on their deep knowledge of your life and your situation, they all agree it would be in your best interest for you to face the consequences of what you've done. After all, it might be the wake-up call you need to get your attention and get you to make needed changes before something even worse happens to you. They'll stick with you through it all, but they won't enable or encourage you to make bad choices.

You don't get to pick and choose when they do this for you. They just do it. They're committed to loving you in a way that sometimes hurts, and you have to have the maturity to see that this is necessary.

If that sounds like something your father or some other family member might do, then you're not far off. There's a difference between friends and family. Your family isn't determined by common interests or similar personalities. If you have a disagreement or get on each other's nerves, you don't stop being family. Your family—especially a parent or a sibling you grew up with every day—knows pretty much everything about you. They've seen you on your good days, your bad days, and every day in-between. And though you might not even *like* your brother or sister, or at least not all the time, you still *love* them. You want what's best for them.

So when I talk about community, I'm talking about people who treat each other as caring family members, even if they're not at all related.

This is exactly the picture God uses when talking about this kind of relationship. Followers of Christ are almost always referred to as "brothers and sisters," with the occasional "father" or "mother" thrown in when talking about believers who are older than you (Matt. 18:15; 25:40; Acts 1:16; 6:3; 11:29; Rom. 7:4; 1 Tim. 5:1–2; Philem. 1:15–16; and many other examples). Jesus, who had literal earthly brothers and sisters, preferred to call his unrelated followers his brothers and sisters (Matt. 12:46–50).

In fact, the only times that God chooses not to use the family metaphor when describing his followers is when he uses an even stronger relationship, referring to us as members of one body (John 15:5; Rom. 12:4–5; 1 Cor. 12:12–27; Col. 1:18; and others). No matter how much you care about your brother or sister, or how connected you are to them, it pales in comparison to how much you care that your heart remains a part of you, or to the level of connection between your arm and your shoulder. The parts of a body literally can't survive without each other. Followers of Christ would be deluded to think that they can survive or thrive without being connected to other members of the body.

Not My Idea

The concept of community isn't something I came up with, and it's not a new or novel idea. God talks about it all the time in Scripture, showing why it's needed, what it involves, and what it's supposed to accomplish.

A few examples:

And let us consider how we may spur one another on toward love and good deeds, not giving up meeting together, as some are in the habit of doing, but encouraging one another—and all the more as you see the Day approaching. (Heb. 10:24–25)

But encourage one another daily, as long as it is called "Today," so that none of you may be hardened by sin's deceitfulness. (Heb. 3:13)

A new command I give you: Love one another. As I have loved you, so you must love one another. By this everyone will know that you are my disciples, if you love one another. (John 13:34–35)

Be devoted to one another in love. Honor one another above yourselves. (Rom. 12:10)

Therefore confess your sins to each other and pray for each other so that you may be healed. The prayer of a righteous person is powerful and effective. (James 5:16)

Carry each other's burdens, and in this way you will fulfill the law of Christ. (Gal. 6:2)

Two are better than one,
  because they have a good return for their labor:
If either of them falls down,
  one can help the other up.
But pity anyone who falls
  and has no one to help them up. (Eccles. 4:9–10)

The way of fools seems right to them,
  but the wise listen to advice. (Prov. 12:15)

Walk with the wise and become wise,
  for a companion of fools suffers harm. (Prov. 13:20)

Wounds from a friend can be trusted,
  but an enemy multiplies kisses. (Prov. 27:6)

As iron sharpens iron,
  so one person sharpens another. (Prov. 27:17)

Remember that anything God asks you to do is done for your own best interests. We're reminded so many times to be in community because it is (A) important, and (B) in your best interest. It's good for you. It's good for you in the same way that exercise or studying is good for you. Exercise and studying aren't always fun, and community can likewise be hard work, but it produces something great in your life.

How to Live Out Community

So what does community look like?

That's a tricky question to answer, because it can take on many forms. But all of those forms should share some things in common.

- For starters, it should be a small group of people. If it's a large group, you can't really get to know everyone deeply. It's the same problem as having a lot of friends. Having just two people would probably be a bit small to call it a "group," although it's infinitely better than nothing.

- Community should be intentional. It rarely happens by accident. You have to be intentionally trying to live out the biblical principles of community, seeking to love each other, help each other, and build each other up as brothers and sisters in Christ.

- You need to meet regularly. You can't really be a part of each other's lives if you rarely see each other or even talk to each other. This is another part of being intentional: unless you're roommates or work together, you'll have to put some effort into seeing each other regularly and communicating about what is going on in your lives. This is an area where you can make technology work in your favor: with phones, group text apps, video chat, and all the other ways we have to communicate from a distance, laziness or lack of caring are the only real excuses you have for not keeping in touch.

- Be open and authentic. This is probably the hardest part for a lot of us who are used to keeping our lives private and hiding our struggles, fears, and mistakes from everyone. Many churches indirectly encourage this by focusing on legalism and rule-following instead of grace and forgiveness. I myself learned to put on a mask and pretend that everything was happy and perfect in my life, even when it most certainly wasn't. But biblical community means being real with each other.

You can't get comfort, help, or advice about what's really bothering you unless you share that with others. Through accepting each other as we are, warts and all, we help demonstrate God's love for us.

- Counsel biblically. In other words, try to give advice based on God's wisdom from the Bible and not just your own opinions or feelings. Your opinion on how someone should handle a given situation may be right, but if so, it will match up with God's opinion, which is always right. We've all heard people give bad advice, and we've probably all unintentionally given bad advice at one time or another. Basing your advice on God's teachings in the Bible avoids that problem.

- The goal is maturity. By "sharpening" one another, you help each other overcome bad habits and change faulty thinking patterns. You become better at navigating decisions in life, both small and large. You become more like the man or woman you were created to be.

Overall, it's about living life together—having people around you and walking through the steps and stages of life together. You rejoice together when it's time to rejoice, and mourn together when it's time to mourn (Rom. 12:15). You are there for each other in everything so that no one has to go through life alone.

Finding Community

What I'm really describing here is church, or what church is supposed to be. It certainly fits with what the early church was like, as described in places like the book of Acts. Back then, no one confused the word *church* with a building, because they hadn't gotten around to constructing church buildings yet. The church was a local group of believers who met together in someone's home and "had everything in common" (Acts 2:44).

Unfortunately, that doesn't describe many churches today. Sometimes that's a function of size: the church I work at and attend has several thousand members, so I can't know every single person deeply.

That's why many large churches like ours emphasize having people form community groups, which are smaller groups of people who can live out community together. They usually meet in their own homes during the week, much like the home-based churches in Acts. You may hear these referred to as home churches, home groups, life groups, small groups, or some other moniker, but all the names essentially mean the same thing.

If your church emphasizes community, all you have to do is take advantage of the resources or training they provide in order to find and form your own band of brothers or sisters.

If that's not the case, then you'll have to take the initiative to create community on your own. Make friends with other believers and discuss this idea of community with them. Start meeting together weekly to study the Bible together, pray together, and discuss what's really going on in your lives.

Over a decade ago, I went to meet with my new community group for the first time. I didn't really know them ahead of time; my church put us together. I awkwardly walked into a house to meet three other guys who all went to the same college, had the same degree, and worked for the same company in the same job. They were pretty much the same person and they could not have been more *different* from me! The conversation dragged on, and I could not wait to get out of there. When the meeting was over, I got in my car and swore I'd never go back.

But I did, for some reason. I went back every Thursday, even when I didn't feel like it. That commitment to those men turned into the single biggest catalyst of growth in my relationship with Jesus. The fact that we were very different was actually good. They learned from me, and I learned much more from them. Ten years later, we still meet every Thursday, and they have become some of my closest friends. Looking back at the past decade together, there have been some really difficult times. We've had times of conflict, times of mourning, and times of separation. However, we've also had a ton of fun. We've traveled together, celebrated together, and shared many meals together, now with families in tow. Without this group of people in my life, I would not even be writing this book.

When forming community, it is a lot easier to do so with people who are your peers and in the same life stage as you are. (You can debate whether "easier" equals "better," but it's definitely easier.) In other words, if you're a single girl in your twenties or thirties, your community would also be single girls in their twenties or thirties. If you're a single guy, look for other single guys. If you're a newly married couple, join up with other newly married couples. At The Porch, we do peer-to-peer community. A more multigenerational approach has some benefits, but it can be very one-sided, more like discipleship than community. As I've said earlier, this discipleship-type relationship is definitely valuable, but we also like to see our young adults thriving in a peer community.

You'll all be going through many of the same changes in life, facing similar struggles, and making similar decisions. You'll be able to help each other as you go through those same things.

It's also easier to open up to such people and be completely honest with them. You're not tempted to filter yourself because you secretly have a crush on the coed across the room. If you're a single guy struggling with a sin such as lust or masturbation, you really wouldn't want to confess that in a coed environment. It's just not conducive to being truly authentic. In married community groups, it might be necessary for the guys and girls to meet separately every so often, for confession and accountability.

If you do find a like-minded group of single guys or girls, consider really digging into each other's lives by moving in together. Some people reading this may think that's extreme, but it's really not. You'll save money, for starters, by sharing the cost of rent. Having a roommate is a great way to prepare for marriage; you learn how to share a living space, share chores, communicate your needs, and make compromises. And, of course, you won't be alone.

Thanks to technology, there are online resources from other churches you can use to help you develop community wherever you are. The church I serve at, Watermark Community Church in Dallas, Texas, has some such resources available. You can visit watermark.org and search for "community group resources" to find messages, online workbooks, and how-to blog posts. They're all free.

But it's not like living life together in community is complicated, requiring a specific formula or a special college degree. It can be hard, yes, but it's not complicated. It's hard because all relationships take work, and we all have human flaws that lead to conflict.

In summary, all you need is a time and a place to meet weekly. Find two to five people who will meet with you. When you meet up, you will divide your time between catching up, confessing sin, celebrating victories, praying together, and sharing what you are learning from God's Word. Avoid giving advice from your opinion; in fact, try to incorporate the discipline of attaching Scripture to any advice you share. Then follow up with each other between meeting times. Check in, encourage, and pray for one another.

Reflection

- What is a bigger temptation for you, hanging out with the wrong people or isolating from everyone?
- How could you improve your commitment to meeting with a group of godly people on a weekly basis for accountability and spiritual growth?
- What is your time, place, and plan for community?

7
Conflict

THE RIGHT WAY TO BE WRONG
(AND VICE VERSA)

My wife is the one who noticed the problem. We didn't even meet each other until college, but she recognized a pattern in the stories I would tell her about my high school days. It seems my stories would often start out with "My best friend Kevin . . ." or "My best friend David . . ." or "My best friend Collin . . ." or "My best friend John . . ."

"How many best friends did you have?!" she asked. Can't you, by definition, only have one friend who is the "best"? How come I had a seemingly endless list of best friends?

The sad answer was that I had a revolving door of "best friends" in high school because I couldn't keep any of them very long. It was definitely my fault; I was the common denominator in all of those relationships. My problem was that I had an anger issue. Something would upset me—usually something fairly minor or small—and I would just explode. It drove people away and ended a number of relationships.

For example, I spent one summer working in a neighboring town, Victoria, wiping down cars at Courtesy Car Wash. Victoria was about thirty miles away from Cuero, where I lived with my parents. So, instead of commuting a half-hour each way every day, I stayed with my best friend, who happened to live in Victoria.

One weekend, some other friends of mine were going to Schlitterbahn. If you live in Texas, you probably already know what that is; it's basically the best water park in the world. I invited the friend I was living with to go along, but he said that he couldn't because he didn't have any money for admission. "No sweat! I got you!" I told him. After all, I did have money—I was making bank at the car wash—and he was letting me live with him for free.

So we all go to Schlitterbahn, and we have an amazing time. That is, we had an amazing time until, on the way out, I see him go into the gift shop and come out with a brand-new puka shell necklace.

This made me angry. Why would a cheap souvenir make me angry? Because he had told me that he didn't have any money, which is why I had paid for his ticket. But clearly he *did* have some money, if he was able to spend it on a puka shell necklace.

I confronted him about it, right there in the Schlitterbahn parking lot. It escalated quickly. Push came to shove, literally. "What are you doing? I thought you didn't have any money!" I said while shoving him backward. It was another explosion of JP's anger. I felt wronged, and in retaliation I tried to embarrass him in front of our friends. It worked; he was embarrassed. But in the process, it cost me a friend. He told me to get my stuff out of his house and leave. That was half a lifetime ago, and things have never really been the same between us. I saw him once, years later, and it was still awkward. I lost an amazing friend because of a minor conflict I didn't handle correctly.

Why We Can't Get Along

Conflict is a fact of life. We're all selfish, sinful people, which means we won't always agree and we will sometimes do things that hurt each other, often unintentionally. So the question isn't whether we'll experience conflict but rather how we'll handle it when it does inevitably happen.

An ability to resolve conflict is one of life's most valuable skills. Since life is so heavily focused on relationships, and relationships always involve conflict, how you resolve those conflicts will have a huge impact on how happy you are. It can even alter the direction of your life in big ways. For example, the number-one predictor of success in marriage is how well the two of you can resolve conflict.[1] An inability to resolve conflict can cost you friends, cost you jobs, and keep you from having peace.

It's a big deal. So big that I've traveled with a group of coworkers to Africa to teach leaders and government officials how to resolve conflict. Presidents of foreign countries have come to our church in Dallas to learn about it. That's not boasting; it's just pointing out the importance of knowing how to resolve conflict. It's something that can change the course of a nation.

At Watermark, our church staff spends most of our time helping people resolve conflict. That should tell you a few things. For starters, it means that conflict happens all the time. It also means that we consider resolving conflict to be important. It's not a distraction from our jobs; it is our jobs. But it also shows that resolving conflict is work.

Anger and Conflict

Occasionally, we may not want to resolve conflict because we like being angry at someone, or because we don't think we could ever forgive them. We feel that our anger is justified. And we figure that as long as we don't *do* anything with that anger—we're not punching them in the face or going out and slashing their tires—then it's really OK to be angry. We're not doing anything wrong. They're the ones who did something wrong.

But that's not how Jesus looked at it. Not at all. In his famous Sermon on the Mount, he had this to say about anger:

> You have heard that it was said to the people long ago, "You shall not murder, and anyone who murders will be subject to judgment." But I tell you that anyone who is angry with a brother or sister will be subject to judgment. Again, anyone who says to a brother or sister, "Raca," is answerable to the court. And anyone who says, "You fool!" will be in danger of the fire of hell. (Matt. 5:21–22)

Whoa, wait a minute. Did he just compare anger to murder? As in, if you're angry with someone, that's equivalent to murdering them?

You don't have to study the Bible to know that murder is wrong. Regardless of belief, everybody knows that murder is not only wrong, it's very wrong. Besides the fact that it ends a life, imagine how it would change your own life if you murdered someone, or someone close to you was murdered. It's a really big deal. And Jesus is saying anger is similar to that? That if I call somebody a fool I'm in danger of the fire of hell?

Yeah, that's what he's saying. Just like when he talks about adultery and lust a few sentences later (vv. 27–28), Jesus is saying that it's your heart that matters, not just your actions. He's not saying you're supposed to be emotionless; Jesus showed plenty of emotion, and it's hard to imagine him overturning tables and driving people out of the temple without displaying at least some temporary anger (John 2:13–17). He's talking about the problem of unresolved anger, as shown by his following sentences:

> Therefore, if you are offering your gift at the altar and there remember that your brother or sister has something against you, leave your gift there in front of the altar. First go and be reconciled to them; then come and offer your gift. (Matt. 5:23–24)

By comparing it to murder, Jesus shows the seriousness of unresolved anger and conflict. And because it's serious, he says you need to do something about it, and do it immediately. Don't wait. Even if you're on the way to present an offering—giving a gift to God—God himself says it's more important for you to resolve that conflict first. He'd rather have you be at peace with your fellow man than receive any offering or act of service you could give. There's nothing you could do that is more important.

Most of us have not taken Jesus seriously here. Imagine how different our lives might be if we did.

Avoiding Conflict

Some people try to handle the problem of conflict by avoiding it completely. But what does that really mean to "avoid conflict"? How does that work in practice? You can't control what other people do, so there's no way to avoid having them do things that hurt you. And though you may try to avoid doing anything yourself that causes conflict with other people, sometimes it happens accidentally: you say or do something with good intentions, but it is interpreted differently by the other person. Conflict will happen. The only surefire way to avoid it completely is to avoid being around other people, living as a hermit in the wilderness.

Even avoiding conflict within just one relationship is difficult. I've heard dating couples say things like, "We have a great relationship. We never argue." This always makes me wonder: Do they even *know* each other? Do they talk about things that matter, or do they only have surface-level conversations? All healthy relationships are marked by conflict. While a relationship that is marked by lots of conflict is not a healthy relationship, a relationship void of any conflict might not be healthy either. If you never disagree at all, or if you do disagree but never discuss it, that's not likely a good sign.

When people say that they avoid conflict, what they really mean is that they avoid conflict *resolution*. They don't resolve the conflict that does come up. They lock it away inside, where it has a tendency to fester and grow. It's like getting a paper cut and then ignoring it: it may heal up and be forgotten, or it may become infected and get worse. It's better to deal with it and clean the wound.

How to Fight Fair

Handling conflict well is all about having good communication. Unfortunately, we all have some negative communication patterns that can lead to conflict or prevent us from resolving it.

There's an acronym we've adapted to make it easy to remember the negative communication patterns so we can catch ourselves when we start to slip into them. The acronym is WENI, and it is based on the patterns described in the book *A Lasting Promise*.[2] It's both a terrible acronym and a great one. I say it's terrible because it doesn't really spell anything, and the one thing it comes closest to spelling is "weenie." But it's also a great acronym because it accomplishes what acronyms are supposed to do: make something easy to remember. When I talk with people in my community group about "not being a weenie," we all know exactly what that means. It's corny and weird, and it works.

The four parts of WENI, or the four negative communication patterns to avoid, are:

Withdrawal

Withdrawal is basically the conflict avoidance mentioned above. It means that when conflict arises, you withdraw. Somebody says something that hurts you, or that you strongly disagree with, and instead of dealing with that issue you back off. You may literally withdraw; you walk out of the room or end the conversation without addressing it. But the problem doesn't go away; you just internalize it and avoid resolving it.

Escalation

Escalation is pretty much the opposite of withdrawal. It's what I was known for among my short-lived friendships in high school. Instead of ignoring what the other person has said or done, you respond by saying or doing something in anger. You raise the stakes and escalate the situation. Someone says something unintentionally hurtful, and you respond with intentionally hurtful words. Someone starts a quiet argument, and you turn it into a shouting match. And then maybe the shouting match escalates into throwing punches. A person who escalates is like a firework stand, just waiting for someone to light a match.

Negative Interpretation

Have you ever said or done something with good (or neutral) intentions, only to have it backfire on you when the other person didn't take it the way you intended? That's what happens with negative interpretation. One person says something seemingly harmless, and the other person interprets it negatively. For example, "You look nice today," which is a pretty straightforward compliment, could be negatively interpreted as meaning that you normally don't look nice and today is just the exception. It might seem silly, but negative interpretation happens all the time.

Invalidation

Invalidation occurs whenever one person denies that the other person has a right to feel the way they feel. If someone gets upset by something you do, and your response is that it's not a big deal and they shouldn't feel upset about it, then you've just invalidated their feelings. You've made (or tried to make) conflict resolution impossible, by denying that there is any conflict to resolve.

We're all guilty of at least one of these four patterns, and we tend to have one or two that we're more prone to slip into. It is important to know which negative communication patterns are a problem for you and then recognize when you are slipping into one so you can quickly stop yourself and prevent the conflict from getting worse.

How to Resolve Conflict

Since conflict is inevitable—and harmful—you need to know how to resolve it.

Jesus himself explains a really simple and clear method we're to use when someone has wronged us. It's recorded in Matthew 18:15–17. Before you even get to the steps listed there, though, there are a couple of things you need to do on your own.

> How can you say to your brother, "Brother, let me take the speck out of your eye," when you yourself fail to see the plank in your own eye? You hypocrite, first take the plank out of your eye, and then you will see clearly to remove the speck from your brother's eye. (Luke 6:42)

First, you need to acknowledge and ask forgiveness for your role in the conflict. It's rare for there to be a conflict that is wholly, 100 percent the other person's fault. Even when it seems like you did nothing wrong to contribute to the problem, carefully consider whether that's the case. Is there anything you could have done differently to prevent the problem or keep it from escalating the way that it did?

This is not at all "blaming the victim." It's just taking responsibility for your own mistakes or sins against your neighbor, assuming there is something to take responsibility for. It might be that the problem is 99 percent the other person's fault. That's fine. Clearly, in that case the other person is almost completely to blame. But take ownership of your 1 percent. Practically, it is much, much easier to get someone to admit they were wrong when you first admit how you were wrong. Own 100 percent of your 1 percent in the conflict.

> A person's wisdom yields patience;
>   it is to one's glory to overlook an offense.
> (Prov. 19:11)

Second, you need to determine whether it's a minor problem that can be overlooked. Some wrongs just aren't that big of a deal. There's no reason we have to make them into a big deal in order to resolve them. If it's a small offense, overlook it.

How do you know if it's small enough to overlook? Basically: if you *can* overlook it, you probably should. If it's something you'll probably just forget about, and if it won't bother you or affect your relationship in any way, then there's no need to pursue it further. However, if it *is* bothering you, even just a little bit, and you don't have peace about it, then you need to go talk with them about it. If you are wondering if it is bothering you, it probably is. Don't call something that is bothering you a "small offense" just because you don't want to put in the work to resolve it.

If you can't overlook it, then you need to talk it out with the person who wronged you. Did you know that the Prince of Peace tells us exactly what to do in this situation?

> If your brother or sister sins, go and point out their fault, just between the two of you. If they listen to you, you have won them over. (Matt. 18:15)

In Matthew 18, Jesus makes it clear how you are to go about this. You start by talking with them one-on-one. This means that there is no attempt to shame them or make them look bad in front of others. You take the problem to the person; you don't gossip about them or complain about what they did to everyone but them. You don't need to "vent" to someone else in order to see if you should go to them. Just go. It's possible that they may not even realize they did anything wrong, so it's not fair when you don't give them a chance to apologize and make it right.

This step might be hard, but it's not complicated. You tell them what they did and how it hurt you, and ask forgiveness for your part in the conflict, if applicable. If they acknowledge that they were wrong and ask for forgiveness, you forgive them. And then you're done; you can move on. In most cases, there is no need to take it any further.

On the other hand, if they won't acknowledge that they have sinned against you and that they need forgiveness, you move on to the next step.

> But if they will not listen, take one or two others along, so that "every matter may be established by the testimony of two or three witnesses." (v. 16)

The next step is to bring others in on the conversation. Take one or two other people with you, and again approach the other person about the problem.

Who should you bring? Either a witness to whatever happened, or, if there is no witness, someone who knows both of you well.

A person might honestly think they didn't do anything wrong. But when confronted by two or three people who all agree that they have done something wrong, a reasonable person would at least consider that the other side may be right.

> If they still refuse to listen, tell it to the church; and if they refuse to listen even to the church, treat them as you would a pagan or a tax collector. (v. 17)

If that doesn't work, and if the person is a believer who is a part of the local church, you bring in church leadership. Basically, you're widening the circle. Instead of just two or three, there are now more people on your side. Hebrews 13:17 tells members of a church to submit to the church leaders' authority, so if you are in conflict with someone who is a Bible-believing Christian, they'll hopefully start to recognize the problem and make amends. If they are not a believer who is part of a church, then there may be nothing more you can do. By the way, do you notice that Jesus seems to expect that every Christian will be involved in a church and under its authority? See also chapter 3!

As Jesus says in Matthew 18:17, if these steps don't work, you are to "treat them as you would a pagan (a nonbeliever) or a tax collector." Now, note that Jesus spent much of his time with sinners, and Matthew himself was once a tax collector.

So this means you should love them, not avoid them or treat them badly.

At this point, even if they have refused to listen, you have peace in knowing that you've done literally everything you could do about it. The fault then lies solely with them.

If it is possible, as far as it depends on you, live at peace with everyone. (Rom. 12:18)

I'm not saying that the process will be a piece of cake. Hard conversations are, well, hard. But they're also not optional. If you're ever going to have peace, you have to resolve conflict.

Conflict as an Opportunity

I used to see conflict as an opportunity to display my anger. I'd been wronged, I would think, so I was justified in being angry at the other person. They deserved whatever was coming as a result of my anger, whether that was harsh words or even a flying fist.

But now I see conflict as a different kind of opportunity. It's an opportunity to show who I belong to.

In the Sermon on the Mount, Jesus says that "Blessed are the peacemakers, for they will be called children of God" (Matt. 5:9).

I have children of my own, and they look quite a bit like me. We share a lot of the same traits. I'm tall, for example, so my kids are pretty tall for their ages. Children take after their parents.

So if we're the children of God, then we should display many of God's traits.

God is the ultimate peacemaker. He was in conflict with the entire human race; every single person ever born has sinned against him. He went to the greatest of lengths to resolve that conflict: he had his Son die on the cross to pay for those sins. It was a really radical thing to do. And because of it, instead of being God's enemies, we're now reconciled to him (Col. 1:21–22).

The way you handle conflict is perhaps your greatest opportunity to show the world that you are a child of God. It should make you stand out; it should be different from how most people in the world handle conflict. It's different because you seek peace. You don't hold grudges. You don't fight or lose your temper. You own your part in creating the conflict, even when it is mostly the other person's fault. You ask forgiveness and offer forgiveness.

People will see that and wonder what makes you different. They may realize that they want the peace you have in your life. And when they ask, you can share with them why you are different and introduce them to your Father.

Reflection

- How can you grow in your ability to see conflict as an opportunity?
- Is your greater temptation fight or flight?
- What unresolved conflicts are in your life right now that you want to deal with?
- Can you commit to talking only to someone who is a part of the problem or the solution?

8
Dating

HAPPILY EVER AFTER?

Thirteen years ago, I stood in the back of a church with my brand-new bride in my arms. We were back at Baylor, her alma mater, and we had just made some crazy promises in front of three hundred of our closest friends and family. Now, however, it was just the two of us. As we stood there in the back of the chapel, I said a prayer for us. As I prayed, I thanked God for allowing me to escape the consequences of my sins. Specifically, my sins in dating. After all, I did not have any STDs, I did not have any children from previous relationships, and I did not have a psychotic ex-girlfriend waiting to kill me after the ceremony. I had made a lot of mistakes in dating, but I'd managed to get away with it.

Or so I thought.

Our first year of marriage was bliss. It's that "honeymoon period" you hear about. We ate out at restaurants, watched movies, and traveled. In year two, though, all that baggage I was carrying from my dating days started to come unpacked. Things went from honeymoon to horrible. The consequences I thought I had avoided were waiting on me. They were worse than STDs, illegitimate children, or psycho exes. I was stuck in a marriage with a woman I had no idea how to love. After years of being enslaved to pornography, I had fed an addiction to variety, so monogamy was a seemingly impossible reality. I felt trapped. Marriage was so different than I thought, and I've learned I'm not alone in that. Every couple my wife and I have since counseled, and those from the dozens of weddings I've officiated, would all attest to the same thing: marriage is challenging, and promiscuity outside of marriage only makes marriage more difficult. Because of the way I had dated, marriage became a prison and a misery I wouldn't wish on anyone, and one which I'd like to spare you from.

Thankfully, that period was also temporary. With a lot of hard work and healing, my wife and I are now in a better place than ever before. But it wasn't a fun process, and there are some different choices I could have made in dating that would have made things a lot easier for us.

The Dating Game

About once a year at The Porch, I'll give a sermon or a series of sermons about dating. And without fail, those will be the highest-attended talks of the entire year. It is the topic to talk about.

Why? Because it's one of the biggest hopes, goals, and thrills for most single adults. But it is also the biggest source of problems for single adults. It causes the most pain, the most heartbreak, the most angst, the most longing, and the most confusion. It's eating everyone's lunch.

The reason that dating causes so many problems is because, by and large, we're all really bad at it. As a society, and as a generation, we're doing it all wrong.

Now, looking at it from the outside, you'd think we would be really good at it. It's the subject of many movies and books, and we have entire TV shows devoted to the "reality" of dating. Based on magazine covers, you should be able to get everything you need to know about dating with one trip through the grocery checkout. We have apps and websites designed to sort through data and help us find the perfect match. We discuss and dissect it endlessly among friends. We start at an early age and get plenty of practice in dating. We should all be experts at this.

The numbers show otherwise. Fewer people are getting married. If you were a young adult in the 1950s, you had better than a 95 percent chance of getting married someday. If you were a young adult in the 1980s, you had about an 86 percent chance of getting married. For young adults today, it is projected that only 75 percent will ever get married, which means that one out of four people will never be married.[1] Those who do get married are tying the knot later in life, taking seven years longer, on average, to find a spouse.[2] Once married, people are far more likely to divorce than in generations past. In 1867, there was only one divorce for every 35.7 marriages. By 1967, there was one divorce for every 3.7 marriages.[3] Since the late 1970s the rate has been about one divorce for every two marriages, or a 50 percent divorce rate.[4] These numbers all show that not only are we bad at dating but we're also rapidly getting worse. We're not as good as our parents were, and not nearly as good as our grandparents were, despite all our seeming advancements.

So where did we go wrong, and how can we make it right?

As a "good Christian," your first instinct might be to go to the Bible and see what it has to say about dating. And the answer is: not much. The Bible doesn't really talk about dating. It certainly never uses the word *dating*, and it rarely gives any examples that in any way resemble what we think of as dating. In fact, the clearest example of a dating relationship in the Bible is probably Samson and Delilah, and that didn't turn out very well for anyone.

So what gives? Dating seems like a very important topic; why doesn't the Bible talk about it more?

The reason is pretty simple: dating as we know it didn't exist when the Bible was written. Dating is a modern invention, and has only been around about a century. God, the inventor of marriage, didn't invent dating. And the "better" we think we are at dating, the worse we are at marriage. This doesn't necessarily mean we need to kiss dating good-bye, but we do need to figure out how God would have us date.

The first thing we have to consider is whether the Bible's relative lack of dating is, in itself, telling us something. It's not like people couldn't date back then. Dating isn't a modern technology that had to be invented. They didn't have computers in Jesus's time because they *couldn't* have computers; they hadn't even "invented" electricity yet. Dating, however, would have been just as possible back then as it is today. There were no technological limitations preventing them from dating. They *chose* not to do it, or at least not to do it the way most people do today. And their results, in terms of successfully creating marriages that would last a lifetime, were far better than the results we get through dating today. You might disagree with my conclusion here, but my point is this: the modern phenomenon of dating has not made us better at marriage.

There are many reasons why our modern take on dating hasn't been successful. In counseling hundreds of young adults (and observing thousands more) who are either single, dating, or engaged, I've noticed a number of common mistakes people make when dating:

- Dating for fun
- Focusing on the physical
- Trying before buying
- Living together
- Treating love as a feeling
- Looking for "the one"
- Thinking that marriage will solve all your problems
- Never asking someone out

Let's look at each of those problems in turn.

Dating for Fun

Why do we date?

The goal of dating is to find the person you're going to marry. Or, at least, that should be the goal. The first problems we run into with modern dating is that some people do it without having marriage as a goal. They date just for fun. To them it's recreation, or perhaps a sport.

What's wrong with that? Well, if your goal is just to have fun, then that is (at most) what you're going to get. You don't always get what you aim for; if I shoot a basketball at a hoop, I'll often miss. However, you'll almost never hit what you're not aiming for. If I shoot a basketball at a wall, then I for sure won't make it in the hoop. If you're not aiming at marriage, then you're very unlikely to find yourself accidentally ending up in a happy, healthy marriage.

So if your goal in dating is to have fun, then sometimes you'll have fun. Sometimes you won't. Even when you do have fun, though, it won't last. All dating relationships either end in marriage or just end. And ending a relationship is never fun. In fact, the more fun you have in a relationship, or the longer that relationship lasts before ending, the more painful that breakup becomes. Dating for fun, therefore, ends up not being very fun at all.

Now, I'm not saying that dating shouldn't be fun. If you are spending time with someone you are eventually going to marry, then I would certainly hope you have fun being around them—because you're going to be around them *a lot*. The difference is that you have an end goal in mind. Your objective is to determine whether this is the person you are going to marry and spend the rest of your life with. If you decide that this is not the person you are going to marry, then you end the relationship at that point. There would be no reason to continue dating each other, because it would not get you any closer to your goal.

This is also why you shouldn't date anyone if you are not ready to be married. If you cannot or are not willing to get married, for whatever reason, then any dating relationship would be doomed to failure. In fact, the better things went, the worse it would be, because it would just make the inevitable breakup more difficult.

Let me say something crazy. If your goal is to get married, you don't actually have to "date" someone to accomplish that. That is why, throughout most of history, people got married without ever really dating.[5] If Facebook had been around hundreds of years ago, there would have been no "dating" relationship status (and certainly none of that "it's complicated" craziness). People were either "single," "engaged," or "married." They were able to skip dating because, first of all, they could observe people around them and see whether someone would make a good husband or wife without ever "dating" them. They also often had family members who could likewise observe and determine who would make a good match for their single relatives. I don't mean to describe a false utopia. Past generations have faced other problems, but when this system works well, it can be beautiful. The thought of "arranged marriages" might seem crazy today, but if we redefine it to mean having family or close friends help you make decisions about whom to date and whom to marry, I'm all for it. If there are people who know you and your prospective mate well, and collectively think you would make a good team, I'd listen.

Focusing on the Physical

I remember one time in high school, during a science class, when the teacher decided to pair students up to work together on a lab project. We didn't get to choose our partners; the teacher randomly picked for us.

I so wanted to be paired up with a particular girl in my class. I'll call her Kelly, both to protect her identity and to pay homage to *Saved by the Bell*. (Think Kelly Kapowski, the girl every guy had a crush on.) Kelly was beautiful, and I thought that being paired with her would be the best thing ever. As the teacher went through the class, announcing lab partners, I kept thinking to myself: *Please pick Kelly. Please, please pick Kelly. Jonathan and Kelly.* The teacher got to my name: "Jonathan . . . and Kelly." Yes! Finally! This was my chance!

There was just one problem: the science teacher was not picking us to go on a prom date together. We were being paired up to do science. Specifically, we were supposed to work together to dissect a frog. Kelly, I quickly learned, thought frogs were gross and cringed at the thought of dissecting anything. She refused to do it. She also, it turned out, wasn't all that smart, at least when it came to the subject of science. Which is a shame, because I (and my grades) really could have used the help. It didn't take long for me to go from wishing I was paired up with Kelly to wishing I had been paired up with pretty much anyone else.

When I hoped to be paired with Kelly, my problem was that I didn't understand the project—or wasn't thinking clearly about it at the time. If I had, I would have wished to be matched up with the smartest, hardest-working person in the class, not the person who was the most physically attractive.

In dating, physical beauty is typically the biggest thing people look for. You might think that makes sense; after all, we're not talking about picking a lab partner, right? No, but you are picking a *life partner*. If your goal in dating is marriage, then you want to pick someone who will be really good at marriage. And believe it or not, how someone looks has almost nothing to do with whether they make a good spouse or not.

Now, it just so happens that I did marry someone who is, as they say, "smokin' hot." But that doesn't negate my point. Because when we have an important decision to make, a disagreement to resolve, or a crisis to negotiate, it's not her beauty that makes me glad I married her. When we have a crying, sick child who's just projectile vomited all over the place, it's not her pretty face or perfectly coiffed hair or fashionable clothing choices that are going to help me defuse the situation and clean up the mess. When the realities of life hit, I don't need a trophy wife; I need someone who can go into battle with me.

Besides, beauty is a depreciating asset. It's the one thing about your future spouse that is guaranteed to fade. People can get smarter, wiser, kinder, and more interesting as decades pass. They can become a better husband or wife. They cannot, however, become younger and prettier. Case in point: when is the last time you were physically attracted to someone in their seventies? If your reason for dating and marrying someone is because they are physically attractive, then you'll no longer have a reason to be married to them in a couple of decades. And if you win someone's attention because of your physical looks, you'll lose their interest for the same reason.

Proverbs 31:30 says that "Charm is deceptive, and beauty is fleeting; but a woman who fears the LORD is to be praised." Though it mentions women specifically, the fact that "beauty is fleeting" applies to men too. We're all getting uglier. And that's OK, as long as you don't make physical beauty your idol or date people primarily because of how they look.

That doesn't mean you can't or shouldn't pursue someone who is physically attractive. There's nothing wrong with marrying someone who happens to be beautiful. But that shouldn't be the main reason why you are attracted to them. "A woman who fears the LORD is to be praised"—and, in the context of Proverbs 31, is someone a man should seek to marry.

I would also say that you should be attracted to your future spouse. But it should be far more than his or her physical aspects that you find attractive. We should seek to see all people the way that God sees them. "The LORD does not look at the things people look at. People look at the outward appearance, but the LORD looks at the heart" (1 Sam. 16:7). I've had people ask me, "What if a particular girl (or guy) is a really godly person, and in every other way would seem like great marriage material, but I'm just not attracted to them? Should I date them anyway?" My answer is no, but that's not because there's anything wrong with the "unattractive" person being described. That person sounds very attractive if you look at them through God's eyes. And if you're not spiritually mature enough to see them that way, then no, you shouldn't be marrying them. But I would pray for God to change your eyes and your heart so that you are attracted to the things that God is attracted to.

Not everyone is a model. And I think that today's world, where we're surrounded by so many people on a daily basis and are easily exposed to altered images of people who already have altered bodies, causes people to focus too much on physical looks. It's easier, after all, to judge someone on physical appearance than it is to get to know them and observe who they really are as a person. With so many apparent options out there, people tend to always be on the lookout for someone prettier or nitpick about small physical preferences. "Oh, well, I want someone taller. Or shorter.

Or thinner. Or with a more athletic build. Or someone with brown eyes instead of blue." In the end, none of those things really matter that much, but they cause you to eliminate or overlook someone who would otherwise be the perfect match.

Trying before Buying

I can't think of anything that has caused more problems and contributed to more pain in dating and marriage than our culture's acceptance of premarital sex.

The idea that it is OK, or even recommended, for people to have sex outside of marriage is a very recent change.[6] In fact, though the "sexual revolution" may have started as a countercultural movement in the 1960s, we're really living in the first generation—ever—in which premarital sex is treated as a normal, nearly universal thing. Most people today expect and assume that singles will have had sex before marriage. It's now considered countercultural when you *don't* treat sex as a standard part of dating.

Some people may even be shocked to hear me suggest that sex shouldn't be a part of dating. But know that if you asked almost anyone at almost any point in history before today, they'd be shocked to hear you suggest that premarital sex is OK.

Have we discovered some new truth that people simply missed out on for thousands of years? Is premarital sex harmless? Is it, as I've heard many people suggest, even helpful, allowing us to make better decisions about who to marry?

The answer is pretty clear when we look at the results.

Some of the potential consequences of premarital sex, such as pregnancy or STDs, are so obvious that it seems almost silly to mention them. Besides, you can eliminate those possibilities if you are careful, right?

Maybe not.

- In the United States, there are still about three million unintended pregnancies each year and over one million abortions. Singles account for about 85 percent of those abortions.[7] This is despite contraception being more widely available than ever and being used in most cases.[8] The majority (51 percent) of these pregnancies occurred despite the use of some form of contraception.[9]

- According to the CDC, there are about nineteen million new cases of sexually transmitted diseases in the United States each year. STDs would be virtually nonexistent if not for sex outside of marriage; if each person had only one partner, they would have no STD to transmit.

When your end goal of dating is marriage, premarital sex presents even more problems. By pretty much every measurement you can think of, marriage is on the decline, and the decline is closely correlated to this rise in premarital sex. In the 1950s, just before the sexual revolution, the average person got married at age twenty-one. (About 21.5 years old, if you want to get more specific.)[10] Today, it's a full seven years older than that, with an average age of twenty-eight (the average was 28.5 in 2017).[11] You're considered an adult and able to make marriage decisions for yourself at age eighteen, which means what used to take three years (eighteen to twenty-one) now takes a full decade (eighteen to twenty-eight).

But at least that extra time spent dating around allows us to find a more compatible spouse and have better marriages, right? Unfortunately, it's the opposite. Studies show that people who have premarital sex are more prone to divorce later on. In fact, having even just one premarital sexual partner makes you about four times more likely to divorce within the first five years of marriage, and having multiple partners results in a divorce rate five to six times higher.[12]

One of the likely reasons for the increase in divorce is because, scientifically speaking, premarital sex causes changes in your body and mind that make marriage more difficult. Sex triggers the release of chemicals such as dopamine, oxytocin, and vasopressin in the brain. These chemicals produce powerful emotional bonds. For example, oxytocin plays a big role in causing mothers to bond with their newborn children. Within marriage, these chemicals help you bond to your spouse, making your marriage stronger. Outside of marriage, they still cause you to bond—but bond with someone who is not your spouse.[13]

These natural chemicals are also addictive. They create passageways in the brain that then become a "path of least resistance" toward that next chemical high. In other words, each time you have sex, it becomes a bit easier to say yes and harder to say no. The same thing happens, by the way, with pornography, which is why so many people become addicted to porn.

So, when you have sex outside of marriage, you are creating that strong bond with the person you're with. But most of the time you don't end up marrying that person. There is a breakup, which is more painful because of the bond. You start seeing someone else, and since you are becoming conditioned to it, you are now more likely to have sex with them—and also bond with them.

The end result is that you slowly lose that ability to chemically bond with your eventual spouse. You become addicted to variety; it's more difficult for you to remain committed to one partner for the rest of your life. Some people claim that is just how humans are, and that we are not wired for monogamy. But the fact that our bodies produce these bonding chemicals proves that we actually are created for monogamy. Our bodies are designed to commit to one person in marriage. We've simply short-circuited that wiring by deciding that we can have sex with a series of partners outside of the commitment of marriage. We sabotage our marriages before they start.[14]

God's intent is for sex to be used only within marriage. Outside of marriage, it causes all these problems. But within a marriage, sex brings life, provides guilt-free enjoyment, and strengthens the bond between husband and wife. It's why Jesus talked about marriage as two people becoming "one flesh," and said that people joined in such a way should not be separated (Mark 10:7–9). And it is probably why God's Word mentions sex outside of marriage more than most other sins and seems to give it special status (1 Cor. 6:18). It's both important and one thing that many people get wrong.

Hey, I'm one of those people. I started having sex in high school, and by college premarital sex had become a sport for me. I became a sex addict. And though it caused me a lot of pain, I want to encourage you that there is hope. I know that, statistically, most of the people reading this will have already had sex before marriage. And although that's not good, it doesn't mean you can't be forgiven, and it doesn't mean your future marriage is doomed. You can start now to change your behavior and your attitude toward sex. It will be real work. It will take time. It will take commitment on your part. It will require daily prayer, confessing the sins of your past and repenting from them, but there is hope and healing ahead for those who seek it. (More on this healing process in the chapters ahead.)

A few people go so far as to use sex to intentionally manipulate people and to try to "trap" someone in a relationship. If this is you, you need to reach out to someone for help. But there is hope for you too.

God is pro-sex. He invented it. He isn't trying to deprive you of anything or keep you from having fun. He wants you to fully enjoy sex and all its benefits—but that can only happen within the context of marriage.

Living Together

Living together before marriage is the ultimate in the "try before you buy" mindset, and it's become so common and so ingrained that it deserves special mention. Depending on which statistic you look at, about two-thirds of young adults now live together before marriage. What would have been a foreign concept a couple of generations ago is now more or less the norm.

Most people who live together before marriage probably think that they're making a wise decision. After all, it seems like this would be a great way to evaluate whether getting married would be a good idea. You're basically living as if you were already married, so if that works for you, surely being married to each other would also work.

There's one big flaw with that line of reasoning: it doesn't work out that way in reality.

Studies have shown for years that people who live together before marriage are actually more likely to divorce after marriage. Such studies also show that married couples who live together first have less marital happiness, poorer communication, and higher levels of abuse.[15]

But that's just the ones who make it to marriage. "Living together before marriage" is kind of a misnomer, because roughly half of all people who cohabitate break up without ever getting married. Because they were living as if they were married, these breakups are quite similar to a divorce, with many of the same hurts and complications. Since about half of those who do get married after living together also get divorced, that's about a 75 percent failure rate for these "trial marriages." Who would want to sign up for those odds?

Because so many people today do cohabitate before marriage, and they don't want to admit that it's a bad idea, I've had people try to argue that somehow all these facts about cohabitation are wrong. Many claim that new research shows that living together before marriage does not hurt your chances after marriage. However, every person I've talked with who has tried to cite "new research" have all referred to only one study: a 2014 article in the *Journal of Marriage and Family*.[16] However, that study actually *also* agrees that people who cohabitate before marriage are more likely to divorce. It simply tries to come up with an argument as to why that is. The argument goes like this:

- People who marry young are more likely to divorce.
- People who cohabitate before marriage are trying to "act married" (their words, not mine) from the moment they first move in together.

- If you pretend those people are married from the moment they move in together, rather than when they actually do get married, that would mean they were "married" at a younger age. And that younger age could explain why their divorce rate is higher.

The most glaring problem with this is that if you're going to say everyone who lives together is already married, you have to also count any cohabitating couple that breaks up as having gotten a divorce. Which, as I've already mentioned, gives you a divorce rate of around 75 percent. Choosing to cohabitate may not guarantee that you'll get a divorce, but it comes fairly close.

Other studies may come along and also try to determine why cohabitation leads to a higher divorce rate and other poor marital outcomes. But remember, the only reason they're able to look for *why* it's higher is because it is, indeed, higher.

So if you want to get married someday and want it to be a happy, successful marriage, one positive step toward that would be to not live together first. Either you're ready to get married to each other or you're not. If you are ready, then just get married; there's no reason to live together first. And if you aren't ready to get married, then you also aren't ready to "act married" by living together. Society may try to say otherwise, but the facts don't lie.

Treating Love as a Feeling

When I first started to date (which was long before I should have), I remember wondering whether I was "in love" with a particular girl. I knew I *liked* her, but did I *love* her? Were my feelings strong enough that they crossed the line into the realm of love? Where was this imaginary line, anyway?

My problem was that I was defining love as a feeling. Though that is one definition of the word, it's not a good thing to base a relationship on. Why? Because feelings change. I could easily feel "in love" with one girl one week, dislike her the next, and then feel "in love" with a completely different girl a few weeks after that. Though I definitely felt "in love" with them at one time, now I have a hard time even remembering their names.

God's Word talks more about love as an action, not a feeling. For example, we're given commands to love others (Mark 12:30–31; John 13:34; Eph. 5:25). You can't command someone to feel a certain way; you can only command them to do something.

Love is also described this way:

> Love is patient, love is kind. It does not envy, it does not boast, it is not proud. It does not dishonor others, it is not self-seeking, it is not easily angered, it keeps no record of wrongs. Love does not delight in evil but rejoices with the truth. It always protects, always trusts, always hopes, always perseveres. (1 Cor. 13:4–7)

All of those are things you do, not things you feel. And that's why verse 8 says that "Love never fails." Feelings would sometimes fail, but since love is an action, you can always love someone regardless of how you might feel at the moment.

I'm not saying that you shouldn't have strong feelings of love for the person you're going to marry. You absolutely should. But I am saying that you need to base your decision on far more than just your feelings. Feelings are real—but they're not reliable. You can feel madly in love with someone who would be a terrible choice for a spouse. (In fact, the very term "madly" in love implies that you've gone mad, and that you're making decisions while not in your right mind.)

Rather than focusing on feelings, let logic guide your decisions. Would this person actually make a good spouse? Since love is an action, do their actions toward you show that they truly love you? Do they live out 1 Corinthians 13? Or do they say the words "I love you" and then prove by their actions that they don't? Do they really just love themselves, and therefore love what you can do for them?

This is where having a community of people around you, people who care for you and want the best for you, can be a huge help. When you have strong feelings for someone, it can be hard to see them clearly. You're biased. You want to believe the best about them. Your close friends or family, however, are *not* in love with the person you're dating. They can see clearly. They do love you (in a nonromantic way), meaning that they want the best for you and truly have your best interests at heart. Involve them in your decision-making and, most importantly, listen to what they say. If you "love" someone, but your closest friends, guided by wisdom and God's Word, think that person is wrong for you, don't ignore their advice.

Looking for "the One"

If you're looking for "the one," or your "soul mate," and you define that as being the one person in all the world who is perfect for you, I have some bad news: they don't exist. You'll never find them. They're off riding unicorns with Bigfoot.

The idea of a soul mate isn't biblical, scientific, or logical. Fact is, there are a number of people who could make a good spouse for you, and you for them.

The reason why this matters is because thinking that you do have a perfect soul mate can lead to some real problems in dating and marriage. In dating, it can keep you single far longer than you need to be—maybe forever. If you're looking for someone who doesn't exist, needless to say you're going to have a really hard time finding them. It can cause you to be too picky, seeing a tiny flaw or minor difference as proof that they're not "the one" for you.

It can also work the other way, causing you to rush into things or stay with someone longer than you should. If you become convinced that someone actually is your soul mate, then you tend to overlook red flags—even major ones. After all, you're meant to be together, right? No, you're not. That's where the warnings about being "madly" in love and not listening to wise counsel come into play.

The idea of a perfect soul mate can also cause problems within marriage. It can cause people to look elsewhere when marriage gets hard, because supposedly if your spouse were "the one," marriage wouldn't require so much work.

No matter how awesome your spouse may be, they're still not going to be perfect. As months and years go by, there will be times when they don't inspire a magical feeling within you. So when you meet someone new, and different, and therefore exciting, there may be a temptation to think that this person is your soul mate. That you somehow got it wrong when you married, and you were meant to end up with this new person instead. And that's wrong. Verifiably wrong, since studies show that people who divorce and then marry someone else don't end up any happier in their new marriage.[17]

Here's how you should look at this concept of there being one person in the whole world who you're meant to be with: the person you marry *is* "the one" for you. But you don't marry them because they're "the one." They become "the one" *because* you're married to them. They're the one you've committed to love for the rest of your life, and the two of you together become one (Mark 10:7–8). They are still the one when they gain weight, lose weight, lose their job, get cancer, or make mistakes. Because that's what true love is. It's not loving someone because they are perfect; that would be easy. It's taking someone who is not perfect and loving them anyway, because that's what you've sworn to do.

Is there someone out there more compatible with Monica (my wife) than I am? Yes! Thousands of men. I am 6'7" and messy. She is 5'3" and rather organized. There are ways in which we're not an obvious match. But she's the one because she's the one I committed to.

If that doesn't sound romantic to you, then you need to change your view of romance. You've been sold a fairy-tale, love-at-first-sight view of love and marriage. It may be cute for cartoons, but you're an adult now, and you live in the real world. To me, it's far more magical to be loved for who I am, flaws and all. I'm not Prince Charming. My bride, as wonderful as she is, is not perfect either. The only perfect person in all of history is Jesus, and he chose to love us—to give his life up for us—even though we are all imperfect, sinful people. He's "The One." And by loving each other as he loves us (1 John 4:19), my wife and I can be "the one" for each other.

Thinking That Marriage Will Solve All Your Problems

Now that I am married, this one almost makes me laugh. You may think, *Once I'm married, I'll no longer struggle with lust.* Or *I'll no longer be jealous of other people who seem to have a perfect life.* Or *I'll no longer have (insert problem here).* Let me be clear: marriage will only make most of these problems grow.

Single people often see marriage as this end-game accomplishment. Once you get married, you're done. You're complete. You've fixed all the problems of singleness.

Except you haven't. Married people have just as many problems as single people. God's Word actually promises that we'll have problems: 1 Corinthians 7:28 says that "those who marry will face many troubles in this life."

Most of these troubles are not new problems, though. I've said before that there really are no "married people problems," there are just "single people problems" that are brought with you into marriage. Marriage amplifies those problems and brings them into clearer focus. For example, I was selfish as a single person, but I wasn't really aware of it. I was used to doing whatever I wanted whenever I wanted and always having things my way. I didn't realize I was being selfish at the time, because there were no one else's needs or wants to consider. When I got married, though, there was suddenly another equal partner in my life. She also wanted things her way, and her way was not the same as mine. I had to learn to compromise. This is a good thing, because it's made me less selfish than I used to be. But it's also made me much more aware of the areas in which I still behave selfishly.

If you're selfish, you'll still be selfish after marriage. If you're unfaithful as a single person, you'll probably be unfaithful once you're married. If you're addicted to pornography, getting married won't cure you. Marriage just makes the consequences more obvious and pronounced.

If people think that getting married will solve their problems, then they'll go into marriage with a lot of problems. They won't work on their issues while they're single, because they see marriage itself as the solution. They, and the people unfortunate enough to marry them, are in for a very rude awakening.

Never Asking

Lastly, one complaint I hear all the time, particularly from single Christian women, is that they never get asked out on a date. They may be great, godly women, and know some great, godly guys, but then those guys never make a move to ask anyone out.

It's one thing to not date because you're not yet ready for marriage. That I support. But if you are otherwise ready for a relationship and the only thing holding you back is fear of rejection—well, welcome to manhood. Initiating things and taking risks is part of being a man. Contrary to popular belief, most girls are not waiting around to laugh in your face when you ask them out. They don't typically respond by turning into a flame-breathing monster who will kill you just for asking. Usually, the worst thing that could happen is that they will say no. That might hurt your ego, sure. But they're just about as likely to say yes. You'll never know which one it is until you ask. If it is a no, you can move on and find someone else to ask. It's better to move on than to always be left wondering.

What You Should Do

I've talked a lot about different dating problems and how we tend to get dating wrong. But how do we fix it? How can we do dating right?

Obviously, it starts with avoiding all the aforementioned mistakes. Don't date just for fun. Don't focus on the physical. Don't sleep together before marriage.

But besides the list of things you *shouldn't* do, there are some positive things you *should* do.

First and foremost, while you are single, make the most of being single. Being single is not a curse. It's not a disease to be cured. You're not in some holding pattern where you can't do anything worthwhile until you get married. The time you spend single—which may be a temporary life stage or could be your whole life—is actually a gift, if you treat it as such. Being single gives you more free time; no matter how busy you think you may be, you're still less busy than you would be with a spouse and kids to take up your time. You also have more freedom in how you use that free time, since you don't have another person's schedule to work around. Want to take a spontaneous road trip with your buddies, go backpacking through Europe, or spend a year doing mission work in Africa? Do it now, while there's nothing stopping you.

Use your free time as a single person to prepare for marriage. The most loving thing you can do for your future spouse, before you even start dating him or her, is to work on yourself first. Break those bad habits that would cause problems within marriage. Recover from past hurts or from mistakes you've made. Start doing the things now that will make you a better spouse in the future. You won't become perfect, so I'm not saying you should wait until you are perfect before pursuing marriage. But get yourself in a good place, where you're not carrying major baggage with you down the wedding aisle.

You shouldn't date if you aren't ready for marriage. But if you have checked your baggage and you are ready for marriage, the next step is figuring out whom to pursue. I tell single guys all the time: find the most godly single woman you know and ask her out. (Not "the most beautiful single woman you know," or even "the most beautiful woman who is at least a little bit godly," but the one who is the godliest.) And if you're a girl who is ready to pursue marriage, and a godly guy does ask you out on a date, say yes. Even if it's not that one guy you've been secretly pining for, or he's not as tall or dark or handsome as you imagined.

With all this talk about dating intentionally for marriage, some might feel the pressure to not waste time with someone until they know they are going to marry. But it's not wasting time if you are both God-fearing people trying to get to know each other better. The pressure's off. You're not deciding whether to get married to each other; it's just one date. Give them a chance, and get to know a little bit more about them other than just how they look on the outside. If you're not interested after one date, there doesn't have to be a second. But you might just be surprised to find that this person is really who you were looking for.

Who to Date

What do I mean when I say to look for a godly man or woman? What does *godly* mean?

I'm talking about dating someone who has the qualities that God says make someone a good spouse. For example, Proverbs 31:10–31 describes a "wife of noble character." From that description, there are a number of character traits you could list that a single man should look for in a potential wife. A woman who displays such traits is "worth far more than rubies," so if you find someone like her, they would be an excellent person to marry.

Proverbs 31 is just one example, though; God's Word is full of wisdom when it comes to choosing a godly wife or husband. If I were to make a list of the top ten things a woman should look for in a potential husband, I'd say you should seek out a man who is (in no particular order):

1. **Honest.** Does he say what he means and do what he says? Does he go out of his way to speak with whole, complete, and concentrated truth? Without honesty, you cannot trust what he says—including when he says he will commit to you in marriage (1 Cor. 13:6).

2. **Kind.** Is he nice to others around him? Don't expect him to be consistently kind to you long-term if he is not kind to others (2 Tim. 2:24).

3. **Selfless.** Does he think of your needs, and the needs of others, ahead of his own? Is he generous and willing to share his possessions and time with others? Husbands are called to love their wives selflessly and sacrificially, "just as Christ loved the church" (Eph. 5:25).

4. **Diligent.** A diligent person can be counted on to provide. Does he work hard (Prov. 12:24)?

5. **Patient.** Is he willing to wait for good things? Does he value you enough to wait for you? *Patient* is the very

first word used to describe love in the famous "love chapter" (1 Cor. 13:4).

6. **Courageous.** Will he stand for what is right when it is difficult, embarrassing, or unpopular? Will he stand up to protect you (1 Cor. 16:13)?

7. **Gentle.** Can he control his strength and balance it with grace (1 Tim. 3:2–3)?

8. **Submissive to authority.** Rebellious guys might grab your heart for a moment, but they will not lead you or themselves well. You want someone who will admit that he is not always right and be willing to change when others point that out to him. Does he listen to others and yield to wisdom (Heb. 13:17)?

9. **Faithful.** This insinuates a reputation. Anyone can fake the things on this list when trying to impress a girl. Does he have a reputation consistent with these character traits (Prov. 20:6)?

10. **Committed to Christ.** Christ should be the focus of his life. This looks like yielding to his Word, being prayerful, living in community, and being committed to a body of believers. If this is there, numbers 1–9 will be too (Gal. 5:22–25).

Similarly, a man should look for a woman who is:

1. **Trustworthy.** Is she dependable? Can you be confident she is going to do what she commits to do (1 Tim. 3:11)?

2. **Modest.** Fearing God means you are more concerned about what he thinks and says than what people think or say. A woman who fears God would dress modestly

rather than show extra skin to get attention from (the wrong kind of) men (1 Pet. 3:3).

3. **Peaceful.** A peaceful woman is not about drama or picking fights but about pursuing and preserving unity (1 Pet. 3:4).

4. **Diligent.** This is actually what much of Proverbs 31 is about: being a hard worker and taking care of what needs to be done, when it needs to be done (Prov. 31:13–18).

5. **Compassionate.** Does she care for those in need (Prov. 31:20)?

6. **Respectful.** It has been said that whereas women need love, men need respect. This is displayed in the way she talks to and about others (Eph. 5:33).

7. **Submissive to authority.** Though some people get upset whenever anyone talks about women being submissive, look again at number 8 on the list of things to look for in a man. Everyone should submit to appropriate authority (1 Pet. 3:1).

8. **Responsible.** Does she plan ahead? Does she handle resources wisely? This idea is all throughout Scripture referring to a wife from the Lord (Prov. 31:21).

9. **Wise.** A wise person makes good decisions and gives good instruction (Prov. 31:26).

10. **Committed to Christ.** This is the same as number 10 on the list of things to look for in a man, and it's equally as important here. If this is there, numbers 1–9 will be there too (Gal. 5:22–25).

While some of these qualities could apply to either sex, and some qualities make both lists, God did create us to play different roles in marriage. There are two lists because Scripture addresses men and women differently. Besides giving you an idea of what you should look for in a spouse, these lists also show you what you should strive to be. Men, if you want to marry a woman who has these godly traits, then you should strive to have the godly traits that she is looking for in a man. Women, if you want a godly man, seek to become a godly woman.

How to Date

When your goal in dating is finding someone to marry, you should go about dating in a way that helps you accomplish that goal. The whole point, in other words, is to get to know the person well enough to make a decision: either yes, we should get married, or no, we should not.

Some people call this "dating intentionally," because you are dating with a purpose and a goal. Of course, some people have "goals" in dating that don't include marriage, but people who talk about "dating intentionally" usually mean dating toward marriage.

Besides having a goal of marriage, I believe an important part of dating intentionally is to be clear about your objective. Dating always involves two people, one of whom is not you. So, you're going to have to communicate to let the other person know what your intentions are.

The key word here is *intentional*, not *intense*. Being intentional doesn't mean discussing your upcoming marriage on the first date. That's a bit weird and really isn't appropriate; it could either set up false expectations or rightfully scare them away. Remember, the goal of a first date is to get to know them and see whether you want to pursue the relationship further.

Actually, that's not just the goal of the first date; that's the goal of *every* date. If you don't want to pursue the relationship further, you should end it. It's like driving down a street with traffic lights at every intersection; if the light is green, you keep going for another block. If they all stay green, then eventually you can be confident you have the green light to marry. But if you come up to a red light—some clear reason why you shouldn't marry each other—the relationship stops. You end the relationship and seek out a new street instead.

I believe that men have a bigger responsibility when it comes to being clear in dating. Men are called to be leaders within marriage (Eph. 5:23; 1 Cor. 11:3), so it makes sense to practice that in a dating relationship. Leaders provide direction and remove confusion. Men, you can do a good job of this by:

- Making it obvious that it is, in fact, a date. Girls, if a guy asks you out, one-on-one, has no business-related agenda, focuses the conversation on learning about you, and pays the bill, that should be enough evidence that it is a date. If he calls soon after to ask you out again, that's a sign he thought it went well.
- If things are going well, ask her out regularly, like once a week. That is way more clear than, say, going on one date in July and then calling her up again after Labor Day. It shows that you are interested in her and that you're serious about building a relationship.
- Defining the relationship. This is such a key part of dating that it's commonly referred to in shorthand slang as "DTR." Defining the relationship may not need to

be a specific event, but if in doubt (or if she seems to be in doubt), clarify your intentions and where you stand.

- If you decide that it's not going to work out, you're going to have to let her know. If you've only been on one date, simply not asking her for a second date should make it clear. But if you've already gone on several dates or have been together for a while, you'll need to say something. Don't just stop asking her out or start ignoring her calls and hope she'll eventually figure it out. Be gentle but clear.

If things go well, as I hope they do, you'll face the decision of whether to get married. Before making those vows, go through premarital counseling at your church or through some other Christian marriage ministry. Marriage is the biggest commitment you can make to another person, and I want you to be clear about what you're agreeing to and have realistic expectations. A good premarital program will also help you think through and talk through important aspects of marriage, such as any plans for raising kids, where you'll spend the holidays, how you'll manage your combined finances, and how you will handle different household chores. Deciding such things before getting married can save you a lot of potential stress, disagreement, or disappointment after marriage.

Staying Single

Statistically, most people reading this will get married someday. However, that doesn't mean everyone will. Some people will choose not to get married because they have no desire to. But some people who do want to get married will end up never walking down the aisle. And to those people, I want to say: it's OK.

It may not seem like it's OK. It may seem like you're missing out and that your life won't be complete. But marriage is not the end goal of life. Marriage doesn't make you complete; you're already complete.

Being single doesn't mean that you are somehow broken or flawed. Jesus was single, and he was perfect. The apostle Paul was also single, and he thought that staying single was a good idea (1 Cor. 7:8).

Marriage does not automatically make someone happier. For every lifelong bachelor or bachelorette who wishes they were married, there is a married person who wishes they were single.

There are benefits to being married, and there are benefits to being single. There are also downsides to each. So wherever you find yourself in life, single or married, make the most of what you have and strive to be content (Phil. 4:11–13).

Reflection

- Do you desire to be married in this season? Why or why not?
- Are you ready to be married in this season? Why or why not?
- Who is the godliest person you know of the opposite sex and do you desire a relationship with them? Why or why not?
- How have you dated poorly in the past?
- What steps will you take to pursue healing from past relationships and bad dating habits?

Adulting
Fearlessly

9
Worry

THE ONLY THING WE HAVE TO FEAR . . .

I once spent a full week writing an email.

It wasn't a super long email; it's not like it took seven days to type it all out. I had it written on day one. But I didn't send it that day. Instead, I read it myself, over and over, looking for ways I could improve it and debating whether I should send it at all.

Having revised it umpteen times and worn myself out worrying about it, I finally sent the email—but not to the people I was writing it for. No, I sent it to some close friends and asked them to read over it and look for any ways to improve it. I wanted reassurance that it was OK to send, that it got my message across in an understandable way, and that I wasn't missing any embarrassing typos.

After a week's worth of edits and revisions, I finally sent the email, for real this time. And after sending it, did I breathe a sigh of relief that it was done? No. I went into my "sent" email folder and reread it *again*, looking for any problems I might have somehow missed, even though at that point it would be impossible to change them. I worried about what kind of response I might get, and then I worried about what I would do if I didn't get any response, and what it might mean if I didn't get a reply.

Why was I so worried about this email? That's the thing: it wasn't anything life-changing. I was sending it to a group of four men who served as my bosses, but it wasn't like they were going to fire me or promote me as a result of that email. It was just an email. But I cared about what these people thought about me. I wanted them to think well of me and wanted to portray myself in a good light through how I wrote that email. I wasted a whole lot of time and caused myself a lot of stress just because I wanted these guys to like me and I thought this email could play a tiny role in that. I was worried but had very little reason to be.

"Worried for no reason" could be my generation's motto. Statistically, we're a worrisome bunch. According to the World Health Organization, America is the most anxious country in the world (or at least ranked number one among the countries they looked at), with one-third of us suffering from an anxiety disorder at some point in our lives.[1] Within this anxious country, young adults are the most anxious of all; more than half of Millennials report that they've lost sleep and lain awake at night in the past month due to stress.[2]

Does it matter? Should we be worried about being worried? It might not seem like a serious problem, but worry—or anxiety or stress or whatever you want to call it—is a big deal. Big enough that we spend a couple billion dollars a year on medications to try to manage it.[3] But you don't have to reach the point of a medical diagnosis for it to impact your health. A large British study of over sixty-eight thousand people found that even low levels of worry could literally kill you. That's right: people with mild symptoms of anxiety, such as sometimes lying awake at night worrying, were 20 percent more likely to die within the ten-year period covered by the study.[4] Remember, loss of sleep is a symptom cited by more than half of all young adults, and that level of anxiety has been shown to kill people. It's taking years off our lives.

Worry isn't just a waste of time; it's a waste of life. Not only is the time we spend worrying unproductive and unpleasant but it negatively impacts our physical health. And those health problems can end up killing you.

If you've experienced trauma or severe anxiety due to chemical imbalances in your brain, this chapter is not meant to treat you but rather to give you some principles that can help point you back to truth and ultimately to hope. Before reading further, please note that I have experienced panic attacks in the middle of the night. I've been faced with racing thoughts and have even sought medical help in a season of severe anxiety. I've continued to return to the truths of God's Word and have found the most freedom in the simple ideas I am sometimes tempted to be cynical toward.

Do Not Be Anxious

For believers, avoiding worry is more than just a good idea. It's the law.

God commands us not to worry. In the Sermon on the Mount, Jesus tells us, "do not worry about your life, what you will eat or drink; or about your body, what you will wear" (Matt. 6:25). To drive home the point, he says the same thing—"do not worry"—three times in that one passage. Similar wording is used in Philippians 4:6: "do not be anxious about anything."

This isn't advice; it's a command. The God who tells us not to murder and not to commit adultery also tells us not to be anxious. Worrying, in other words, is a sin. Don't let that label cause further guilt to your anxious mind; read on.

You might think, *But I can't help it. Murder is an act of will; my worrying is not.* That can't be true, though. God would not make it where you have to sin, and we've already established that worrying is sin. You can choose not to worry and choose to trust God instead.

Why would God care whether we worry or not? Remember, God has your best interests in mind. He's not trying to spoil your fun; if something is a sin, it's because that thing is not good for you in the long run. Worrying is both not fun and not good for you. As Jesus says in Matthew 6:27, "Can any one of you by worrying add a single hour to your life?" He knew what modern science now confirms: worrying shortens your lifespan.

But there's more to it than just the health costs. Worrying is not just a cause of problems; it's a symptom of a deeper problem.

Who's in Control?

When my firstborn, Presley, was younger, we would go to the grocery store together and I would use the cart with the car on front and let her "drive." You know, the bright, plastic cars on the front of some shopping carts that give kids a place to sit while their parents shop? It has a steering wheel that doesn't actually steer anything. We had a lot of fun as I'd watch her turn the wheel left or right and then push the cart in the direction she wanted to go. She would laugh as she thought she was driving and enjoyed operating under the illusion of control. Of course, I was the one pushing the cart as she drove us into the apples or caused us to bump into the cereal. I went wherever she steered.

Eventually, however, Presley would turn the wheel one direction but I would take us the other way. As I steered us left, she would become frustrated and grip the wheel and with all her might turn it right. Effortlessly, I continued to take us left to get done what we needed to get done. After all, I had a grocery list I needed to knock out. We weren't there to play; the purpose of the trip was to get the food and other items we needed from the store. Her random "driving" was not going to get us down all the aisles we needed to visit. The game had to end at some point. Her illusion of controlling the cart's direction was gone. She'd never actually been in control at all.

I think that provides a pretty good picture of how we, as adults, become stressed and worried over the issue of control. We only worry about things out of our control or about things we don't feel confident we can control correctly. Worry is always directly related to control, because if we fully trust whoever has control over our situation, we would have no reason to worry about what will happen. The problem comes when we either don't know who is in control or don't trust the one who is driving. Think about it:

- If you believe you are driving and are the one in control of your situation, then you will worry if you do not fully trust in your ability to produce the outcome you want. You might not make that sale or might screw up that date with "the one."
- If you believe that no one is driving, and life is all random chance, then you probably should be worried, because anything could happen at any time for no reason at all. You have no control, and neither does anyone else.
- If you believe that God is driving, and you still find yourself worrying, then you are not trusting that his plan is actually in your best interests.

The first option, where you are the one in control, is actually part of most religions: the idea that your eternal fate depends on you successfully doing or not doing certain things. Since you can mess up at any time and might not have a chance to make it right, you can never be free from worry.

The second option is at the core of the atheist worldview. There is no control, and life is like one big game of roulette. Your greatest hope is "good luck." If that's your worldview, you actually have very good reason to be anxious. I'd be worried too.

In my opinion, though, the third source of worry is the most troublesome one. It would mean you believe that God has a plan, but that plan is to harm you, and that God is in control of everything, but the fact that he's in control is a source of worry. Plus, since God says quite clearly that his plans for you are good, that would make him out to be a cruel liar.

Pretending to offer what is good, while secretly setting you up for harm, doesn't sound like God at all. In fact, that sounds pretty much exactly like the enemy. You're not believing God; you're believing Satan's lies. Satan's MO, even from the Garden of Eden, has been to convince people that God is not good and that we should be the ones in control.

The truth is that God is in control, and he is good. He wants what is best for us. His power is infinite, and he loves us. Since he is completely in control and completely loves us, we can trust him in unemployment, late projects, break-ups, singleness, sickness, and even death. "In all things God works for the good of those who love him" (Rom. 8:28). It might not appear that way in the short term, and our nearsightedness might make it seem like a certain situation could never end up resulting in anything good, but we can only see the here and now. God sees everything, from the beginning to the end, and he already knows what the end result is going to be. History is full of redemption stories that must at one point have seemed impossible to the people living through them, but which God ultimately used for good.

Tim Keller put it succinctly: "Worry is not believing God will get it right, and bitterness is believing God got it wrong."[5]

Pause to consider this very powerful equation:

God is in control + God is good + God loves you = Your peace

Trust Issues

Most of our worries aren't really worth worrying about. Even if they do happen, they're not actually all that bad. By worrying, we build them up into something they're not. Consider how few of the things you've worried about throughout the years have actually come to fruition. Ask yourself, *How many times have I worried about something that never happened?*

I remember being in sales and worrying about whether I was going to make my sales quota one month. A good friend challenged me. "So what if you don't make your quota? What would be so bad about that?" he asked. "Well," I said, "if I miss my quota too many times, I might lose my job. And if I lose my job, I might not be able to get another job. And if I can't get another job, I won't have any money. And if I don't have any money, I won't be able to get a date. And if I don't get any dates, I'll never get married. And if I never get married, I'll live alone. And if I live alone, I'll end up with lots of cats. And I don't even like cats."

Add up all the "ifs," and you're just about as likely to win the lottery as you are to see your fears come true.

Or how about this one: "If I lose my job, I won't have any money, and I'll starve to death." Really? Starve to death? Today? In America? God has expressly promised his followers, in Matthew 6:30–33, that we'll have food and clothing if we simply seek after him. If somehow that worry did happen, and you did starve to death, can you imagine the conversation in heaven? "God, what were you thinking, letting me starve to death down there?! Also, wow! Heaven is incredible!" The way I see it, I guess if you starve to death pursuing the Lord, you win!

You see, no matter how bad things are, they aren't actually that bad.

In reality, though, we're not that worried about starving to death. We're worried about our comfort level. We're afraid that we might have to truly trust in God rather than trusting in ourselves. We'd rather not have to rely on the faith we say we have. We'll trust God for our eternal salvation, but not trust him in the small details of our day-to-day life? That's not really trust.

Worrying is really a form of idol worship. We don't think much today about the commands not to worship idols, because we associate that with bowing down to little statues and false gods. But an idol is anything that becomes too important in your life. If you're more concerned about what other people think of you than what God thinks about you, then the approval of others is an idol for you. If you trust in your bank account for security rather than trusting in God, then money is an idol for you.

Basically, show me what you're worried about and I will show you your idols. A person who fully trusts in God would have no reason to worry.

Waging War on Worry

OK, so you know that anxiety is a problem—which means you might now be worried about the fact that you are worried. *Thanks, JP, you made the problem worse.*

So how do you stop worrying?

The source of anxiety is a lack of trust in the One who is in control. The solution, therefore, is to learn to trust him more.

You have to fight the two lies at the root of worry: that God is not in control and that God is not good. If you trust that God is in control and that he has your best interests in mind, you won't have anything to worry about.

I'm not saying it's easy. It's an ongoing internal battle you have to fight. Second Corinthians 10:5 says that "We demolish arguments and every pretension that sets itself up against the knowledge of God, and we take captive every thought to make it obedient to Christ." The ideas that God is not in control and that he is not good are arguments that go against the knowledge of who God is and what he has promised through his Word. We are supposed to "demolish" those arguments and "take captive every thought to make it obedient." Those are forceful words. Those are words of war.

A few years ago, I discovered that I had a serious rat problem in my house. Rats had taken up residence in the attic and, finding it somehow preferable to all the other attics in town, invited all their friends over to form a giant rat commune. If rats had a Craigslist, I'm sure it would have been filled with ads to come live at my house. "Free rent," they'd say. "Fully stocked pantry. Owner doesn't like cats."

It was such a big problem that I called in a "professional" rat exterminator. I spent a lot of money for his services. But despite all that money and all his tools, he couldn't solve the problem. We were still overrun with rats. He said there were hundreds of them.

So I declared war on rats myself. I went to the store and spent $1.87 on a rat trap. I baited it with peanut butter and bacon bits, which I'd heard works far better than cheese. I waited until I heard the *snap* sound of the trap being triggered. Then I retrieved the trap, got rid of the rat, and set the trap again with more peanut butter and bacon bits. *Snap!* Do it again. *Snap!* Do it again. And again. And again. And again. Until weeks later, after I set the trap again and waited, I heard nothing. The trap sat there for days and was never triggered, because there weren't any rats left to be caught in it. Victory was mine. I killed every rat in Dallas. You're welcome. It's a great place to live now, if you happen to be looking. No rats.

The point is, the way you win this war is through a whole lot of little daily battles. Like the rats, you have to take your worrisome thoughts captive. What if I don't make quota this month? *Snap!* What if I don't pass the test? *Snap!* What if I make a fool of myself in this interview? *Snap!* What if she doesn't like me? *Snap!* What if I lose my job? *Snap!* What if I don't have any money? *Snap!*

Replace those thoughts with the truth. What if I don't make quota this month? *Well, then, I don't. And I move on to next month.* What if I don't pass the test? *Then I'll probably have to retake it.* What if I make a fool of myself in this interview? *Then I probably won't get the job, which means this job wasn't meant for me. I'll have to seek out a different job.* What if she doesn't like me? *Then she doesn't. Not everyone has to like me. I'll move on.*

Some of you might be thinking that your worries are much more severe than the examples here. Please don't feel hopeless; this is where a healthy church can really help you. I'd encourage you to lean into your church leaders and community for help and healing, and keep reading as we discuss recovery in the next chapter.

Regardless of what happens, God is in control. I can trust that he's working everything out for good.

Along with taking thoughts captive, try to take things one day at a time. Matthew 6:34 says, "Therefore do not worry about tomorrow, for tomorrow will worry about itself. Each day has enough trouble of its own." It doesn't do any good to be anxious about something that's in the future and that you can't do anything about right now.

Be nearsighted with your worries, not farsighted. Here's what I mean: I believe Jesus is telling us to give our worries a twelve-hour boundary. If it's not going to happen in the next twelve hours, don't worry about it.

This doesn't mean you don't take action or plan ahead. If I need to make quota this month, I'm not going to wait until the last day of the month to start working toward that. I'm going to work diligently every day, but I'm going to focus on just that day. Do what you need to do that day. Spending your day worrying is counterproductive, anyway. It makes you less likely to reach your goals. By avoiding worry, you're more likely to avoid the consequence you were worrying about.

Lastly, remember God's credentials.

In my twenties, I was terrified to fly. The night before getting on a plane, I'd lie in bed and feel waves of anxiety overtake me in anticipation of the next day. One day I was flying from Dallas to Miami. As the plane took off, my palms were sweaty and my chest felt like it was about to cave in. As we got in the air, I began counting my breaths with my eyes closed and pleading with God to hold us in the sky. We hit some turbulence, the plane began to move around, and I could feel sweat roll down my forehead. I watched the flight attendants closely to see if they were nervous. We hit a big pocket of air and the plane dropped suddenly, with a huge jolt. My Bible bounced off the ceiling. The guy in front of me had coffee all over him. The grandmother behind me began to pray with her two grandchildren. Without thinking about it I turned around and grabbed her hand. She opened one eye to see who it was and I gave her a "keep-praying-lady" look. It's crazy what you think and do when you are given to fear. I began to think,

I'm safe. I love God, so he wouldn't kill me like this, right?
Then, I looked around and realized our plane was full of
college students on spring break, headed to party in Miami.
*What if God's wrath is reserved for them and I'm collateral
damage? What if my wife and I got on the wrong plane?!*
I thought.

Listen, I know God loves wild spring breakers, one of
which I once was. I am just intending to show you how ridiculous our thoughts can get in these moments of intense
anxiety.

I hated everything about flying. Even the airport was a
stressful place for me. When I was growing up, our family
didn't travel much, so I wasn't used to the whole process.
Everyone else in the airport seemed to know exactly what
to do and where to go, while I felt like a fish out of water.
On the plane was even worse. I'd fold my 6'7" self into the
little seat and pretty much hyperventilate until we landed.
I'd feel every bump. Every noise would increase my anxiety.

One day I sat beside a pilot who happened to be a pas-
senger on the flight. He sensed I was nervous and began to
tell me how safe flying was. He explained how the plane had
plenty of lift and lots of redundant safety measures. I told
him that it was a control thing. I literally would rather be
the one flying the plane, instead of the pilot who was trained
to fly it, just so I would be in control. He began to tell me
how "trained" they actually were. "Those guys are retired
military veterans who are used to flying jets at Mach speeds
while dodging enemies. They could do this in their sleep. The
only time they are probably having fun is in the turbulence."
What?! Turbulence was fun?! I began to notice the age of the
pilots. I noticed their grey hair and the stripes and badges

on their uniforms. I thought about their qualifications and experience.

While thinking about how qualified the pilot was brought some peace, considering how experienced God is really gave me peace. God has parted seas, stopped the sun, killed giants with stones, kept people safe in a furnace, shut the mouths of lions, and preserved life inside a whale's stomach. God has healed the sick and made the blind see, the deaf hear, the lame walk, and the mute speak. God has even brought the dead back to life! And he is at the wheel. What am I to be anxious about? Besides, if you die in a plane crash as a follower of Jesus—you win!

Worrying is a waste of time and a waste of life. Don't waste your life.

Reflection

- What are you most worried about today?
- How does your lack of control correlate to the things that cause you anxiety?
- How are you doing at the practice of taking your thoughts captive?
- How can you grow in your ability to trust that God is in control?

10
Recovery

LEAVING THE PAST BEHIND

Amy Winehouse has been called the most talented singer of my generation.[1] In 2008, when she was just twenty-four years old, she won five Grammy Awards; at that time, no female artist had ever won more of the awards in a single night. She won the Grammy Award for Best New Artist, beating out Taylor Swift, and also won Best Pop Vocal Album. The other three awards were all for her signature song, "Rehab," a catchy, strangely upbeat song she wrote about her own life. The lyrics consist of the singer repeatedly refusing to go to rehab, even though the people around her try to get her to go.

While many songs tell made-up stories or use personal experiences to speak broadly about general themes of love or loss, "Rehab" is both autobiographical and specific. Amy's heavy use of drugs and alcohol were well-known and were already negatively affecting her career and her health. Her management company did try to make her go to rehab, but she refused. Likewise, her dad, who once agreed with her that she was "fine" and didn't need help, eventually also tried to make her go to rehab. She wouldn't go. Or rather, she said that she did, but "for just 15 minutes."[2] A full stint in rehab is ten weeks, or seventy days, both of which she references in the lyrics, but she said that she didn't have the time for a ten-week program.

Tragically, Amy's issues eventually caught up to her. She died in 2011, at the young age of twenty-seven, due to alcohol poisoning. Her family and friends were robbed of her presence, and the world lost a great talent, due to the addictions she couldn't control on her own. The girl who once sang that she didn't have the time to spend ten weeks getting help and getting healed lost decades of her life as a result.

As the old saying goes, "There but for the grace of God go I." I'm not criticizing Amy Winehouse, because I've done some of the things she has. (The drug and alcohol things; not the crazy-talented and successful singer things.) Perhaps you have too, though hopefully not to the same extent. Even if you can't relate to her specific struggles, I know you have struggles of your own: perhaps it's lust or pornography or materialism or control or body image or abuse. Or maybe you think you have no problems and are perfect, in which case your problem is pride.

Some addictions can literally kill you if you take them too far; others may seem relatively harmless in comparison. But even if your particular struggle doesn't physically kill you when you overdose on it, it can still bring death: death to your relationships, your career, your happiness, or your effectiveness for God. Be thankful that it hasn't killed you, but do something about the problem before it gets the chance.

One of my goals for this book is to help you avoid becoming trapped by sin and enslaved by addiction. I'd rather you not need to go through rehab. But, in a way, we all need to be rehabilitated. We all sin, and we all have a natural tendency to fall into destructive patterns. For some of us, those sin patterns lead us into substance abuse and other addictions, sometimes to the extent that you might literally need to go into a ten-week rehab program. If that's you, go; you can't afford not to. But for everyone else, you still need help, and that help is available. Even if you think this doesn't apply to you, keep reading.

Houston, We Do Have a Problem

I probably have the worst eating habits of anyone I know.

Every morning, when I wake up, I crave chocolate. Weird, I know. Most people crave coffee or bacon or other breakfast foods; I want chocolate in the mornings. So I'll often have a Hershey's bar for breakfast. Not a Snickers or an Almond Joy or something that at least has some nuts or some other ingredients in it; just a regular, chocolate-only Hershey's bar.

We're also a dessert family. We love all kinds of dessert: cakes, cookies, pies, candy, sundaes, or whatever. If it's on a dessert menu, we're a fan. I'll sometimes take the kids to get frozen yogurt and pretend that it's a treat for them, but really I'm going to satisfy my own sweet tooth.

Plus, I have no idea why, but around midnight every single day, ice cream starts sounding really good to me. So I always keep some in the freezer for a late-night snack. Blue Bell, of course, since I'm from Texas. Only the best.

I never really figured any of this was a problem. After all, it's not like I was noticeably fat. I'm in the weird-tall category, so there's a lot of room to hide such things.

Then, when I turned thirty years old, I had a kidney stone. I spent my thirtieth birthday at the hospital. Part of the diagnosis involved having a CAT scan. While looking at the results of the scan, the doctor asked me, "Do you know that you have a fatty liver?" Uh, no, I didn't. I didn't even know that was a thing. I knew I had a liver in there, somewhere, but I didn't know it could be "fatty," or whether that was a bad thing. I asked her what that meant and whether it was important. She said that it meant I was prediabetic. That made sense; my dad has diabetes, so it wasn't a big surprise that I would be prediabetic. But I didn't think it was a big deal. She talked like it was really serious, but I figured she was paid to do that. She was supposed to point out every little thing.

Not long after that, I traveled to my hometown to visit my parents. While there, I ran into an old friend of mine. In talking to her, I found out that her dad had died. Of course, I was very sorry to hear that and gave her my condolences. Her dad was relatively young; just my parents' age. So, later that night, I asked my parents what had happened to him and whether they knew how he had died. My mom said, "Well, he had diabetes." I said, "Oh, OK, I didn't know he had diabetes. But how did he die?" She replied, "He died from diabetes." "You can die from diabetes?!"

I didn't know that was even possible.

I realized I'd never researched the disease and didn't know what it could do to your body. So I looked it up online. And I learned that diabetes can lead to blindness, heart disease, stroke, kidney failure, amputations, nerve damage, and death. That's a really severe list of potential consequences. Suddenly, being prediabetic seemed like a really big deal after all. I realized I needed to make some changes. No more chocolate for breakfast. Time to cut way back on desserts. It turns out my little Blue Bell habit could kill me.

Now, if you'd asked me before that what my biggest sin struggles, bad habits, or addictions might be, "chocolate" would not have made it into my top ten list. It didn't even cross my mind that it was a problem. Overindulging on sugar is not something that people typically think of as a sin, and gluttony is not something that gets preached about much on Sunday mornings. But that didn't make my problem any less serious.

Perhaps you think your problem isn't really a problem. It's nothing serious; you can live with it. It's not something you need to bother getting help for. After all, you're so much better than those other people, the people with problems that you normally associate with rehab. In comparison, your problem is hardly even worth mentioning.

That's what I thought about my cute little sugar habit, but I was wrong. I possibly could have even been dead wrong, if God hadn't used my circumstances to show me differently.

So don't minimize for yourself the importance or severity of anything that God calls "sin." No sin is harmless, and it's certainly not helpful. Nobody's ever felt better about themselves or been healthier or had a closer relationship with God as a result of doing something they know is a sin. It has zero positive benefits. It can only do harm. And if you choose to go on harming yourself—over and over and over again—well, that's not a minor problem. It's something worth getting help for.

In Jesus's time, there was a group of people who were known for having it all together. They were called Pharisees. Their defining trait was that they followed all the rules, even the tiniest and most obscure ones. They were, literally, holier than thou. And that was really their point: they wanted you to think that they were better than you. Admitting publicly that they had flaws, and were less than perfect, would ruin their image and defeat the whole point of the show they were putting on.

And what did Jesus think of the Pharisees? Did he like them better because they were closer to perfect, and didn't have any of the big, obvious sins like the thieves and drunkards and prostitutes in the community? Not at all. In fact, Jesus spent most of his time hanging out with and healing "sinners"—people with obvious problems who admitted they needed help—while he had harsh words for the Pharisees (Matt. 9:10–13; 23:1–39). He was gentle with those who realized they had problems and practiced tough love with people who thought they were already good enough.

Don't be a Pharisee. You're not perfect, and that's OK. Jesus is here to help.

The First Step

Much of what I have to say on this topic is really just repeating what I've heard said by my close friend, coworker, and community group member, John Elmore. John is the leader of re:generation, one of the largest recovery ministries in the world. Re:generation is a twelve-step program that can help you recover from almost anything, from pride to pornography addiction to alcoholism to materialism.

There are a number of twelve-step programs out there. Besides Alcoholics Anonymous and Narcotics Anonymous, there are at least thirty other "Anonymous" recovery programs dealing with specific issues, plus more general church-based programs like Celebrate Recovery and re:generation. They all use twelve steps, and though the steps might vary a little between programs, the first step is always the same. In fact, it's so common that you've probably heard it referenced in popular culture: the first step is to admit that you have a problem. Or, more specifically, "We admit that we are powerless over our addictions."

In other words, you need to realize that you can't fix the problem on your own and that you need outside help.

There's a reason why this is the first step. Until you admit that there is a problem, you won't do anything to resolve that problem (because, in your mind, there's no problem to be solved). If you don't admit that you need to get help, then you'll never try to get help.

Most people are reluctant to admit they need help. No one likes being "powerless," especially over their own actions and choices. Perhaps that's you, right now. You recognize you have a problem, but you think you can handle it. Sure, you haven't managed to quit yet, but all you have to do is try harder. Have more willpower. *Really* mean it this time.

You know the definition of insanity? It's doing the same thing over and over again and expecting different results.

Look, I understand not wanting to admit you need help and literally *can't* do it on your own. It feels like admitting defeat. It feels like admitting there is something fundamentally wrong with you, since you can't stop sinning on your own. But the thing is, there *is* something fundamentally wrong with you. There's something wrong with all of us. We're all sinners, whether we want to be or not. It's part of human nature. And admitting you need help and can't be perfect on your own is not merely the first step of rehab. It's the first step in becoming a Christian at all. Following Jesus means admitting you are a sinner who needs saving, you can't be made right on your own, and you desperately need help. Accepting help doesn't make you less of a Christian; it's what makes you a Christian.

> I am unspiritual, sold as a slave to sin. I do not understand what I do. For what I want to do I do not do, but what I hate I do. . . . I have the desire to do what is good, but I cannot carry it out. For I do not do the good I want to do, but the evil I do not want to do—this I keep on doing. (Rom. 7:14–15, 18–19)

The quote above was not written by a crazy person, or by the world's most hopeless addict. It was written by the apostle Paul. Now, Paul was not just an ordinary Christian. He was, you could argue, the greatest Christian to have ever lived, or at least the most important. (Jesus isn't in the running for that title because he wasn't a Christian; he was Christ himself.) Paul wrote most of the New Testament and did more to spread the gospel than just about anyone else in history. After becoming a Christian, he dedicated the remainder of his life to that mission and was eventually jailed and martyred because of it.

Yet even Paul, the super-Christian, talked about sin as something he couldn't control and couldn't overcome on his own. He wanted to stop sinning but he *couldn't*. It was impossible for him to do without help. And if Paul is OK with saying that, I think it's OK for me to admit it too.

Where to Get Help

Once you recognize that you need help, where are you supposed to get help? From the same place Paul got help in Romans 7:

> What a wretched man I am! Who will rescue me from this body that is subject to death? Thanks be to God, who delivers me through Jesus Christ our Lord! (vv. 24–25)

God is the only One powerful enough to break the power of sin over your life.

This is the second step in any twelve-step program. The first step is to admit; the second step is to believe. Believe that God is the One who can restore you.

Note that this is step two not only in explicitly Christian programs like re:generation but also in secular twelve-step programs. They may refrain from saying "Jesus" or even "God," referring to a generic "higher power" instead, but they still acknowledge that this is the only way to get free. God is the Higher Power, and he is the only One who can break the power of sin over your life.

When we try to do it on our own, it's because we want to be our own god. But when we let Jesus be Lord over our lives we find healing, saying, "I can't, but God can. I'm powerless; he's powerful."

If we turn to anything other than God, then we tend to just swap one sin for another. We trade an addiction to pornography for an addiction to some other kind of drug, or stop wasting our lives on video games because we're too busy wasting our lives watching TV. There's always going to be a hole in your life that you're trying to fill, a pain you're trying to forget, or an insecurity you're trying to secure. The solution isn't going to come from putting a Band-Aid on it. The solution is to let God heal what's wrong.

Trust God

I promise I won't go through all twelve steps here, but there is one more worth mentioning. Step three is trust: we decide to trust God with our lives and wills.

If you've already trusted in Jesus as Lord, then this step is really just the process of living that out. It's not a one-time decision; every day, and every moment, you have the choice to either trust God or not.

When I talk about overcoming sin patterns and addictions, I'm not aiming for behavior modification. I'm not interested in getting you to just change your behavior. I do want what's best for you, and if you have a behavior that is causing you harm, then I do want you to stop harming yourself. But, as I've mentioned before, life is not about following the rules or "being good." It's about what you believe.

But what you believe and how you behave are inextricably linked. Your behavior *always* follows your beliefs. Here's what I mean: if you do something—anything—it is because you believe that thing will bring you life. You believe that doing it will somehow make you happier than if you did not do it. And if you choose *not* to do something, it's because you believe it will not bring you life.

For example, we all believe that touching a hot stove will bring us pain. That red glow or blue flame might look nice, but it will not bring happiness if we touch it. Some of us learned that the hard way, as kids, by touching a hot stove and experiencing the pain firsthand. But some of us did not. Some of us were warned by our parents that it would be painful, and because we trusted our parents and knew that they had our best interests in mind, we believed them. Whether through experience or through trust, we believe that touching a hot stove will bring us pain. So we don't do it. In fact, you couldn't pay me to touch a hot stove. If you tried to make me do it, you'd have to be bigger and stronger than I was, because I'd fight you to keep from having to touch it. My behavior in regard to the stove is completely determined by my belief.

My behavior in regard to chocolate was, for most of my life, the opposite. I always went for the chocolate. I never avoided it. That's because I believed that eating chocolate would bring me joy. And it typically did—in the short term. But once I learned that my behavior in regard to sweets was not going to improve my life long-term—that it actually might *end* my life if I ate too much of it—my behavior changed. If I believe that something will harm me and rob me of long-term joy, my behavior will change as a result of that belief.

As Christians, we say that we trust God and believe in his promises. However, our actions sometimes show otherwise. We do things that God clearly says are bad for us, or fail to do things that he asks us to do. This doesn't necessarily mean we don't believe in or trust God, but it does show we're not believing him in that moment or trusting him in that area of our lives. We know God says it will be better for us to abstain from that particular sin, but we don't believe that's actually true. We think he's holding out on us. We see God as some kind of cosmic killjoy who is trying to keep us from having fun.

Not only is this not true, it's actually the opposite of the truth: what God wants for us is the most joy and the least pain. That's why he warns us away from certain actions and encourages us to do other things instead. But since the beginning, Satan's MO has been to convince us that God doesn't have our best interests in mind and that God is preventing us from having what we want. It's the way the enemy usually works, not through obvious acts of ugly evil but through little whispers of "It's not really bad for you," or "It's no big deal if you do it this once," or "You've already done it once, so you might as well do it again."

Similar to the battle against worry, the solution is to combat these little lies with the truth, trusting that God really does know what's best for you.

After trusting in Christ in my twenties, there were a lot of changes I needed to make in my life and a lot of bad habits I had to break. It seemed like a huge challenge at first. But then I started doing something really simple: every time I faced a decision about what to do, I would ask myself, *What does God have to say about this?* And then I would do what he said. I would trust that God knew what was best for me. It was a nearly constant conversation with myself. If I had a desire to look at pornography, I'd ask what God had to say about that. *He says no pornography? OK, then*

I won't do that. A buddy wants to hang out and have a few drinks. What does God have to say about that? He doesn't say that it's wrong to drink alcohol, but he does say in the Bible that you shouldn't get drunk. OK, *so I might have one drink, if I want, but I'll stop at one.* And so on and so forth. Every decision, every day. It might sound exhausting, but it was actually quite freeing. I didn't have to wrestle over decisions of what I was going to do or how I was going to handle different situations. I just trusted in God and did what he said.

I quickly realized that, in the vast majority of decisions, God gives us the freedom to do what we want. Following him is not restrictive. It frees us from the consequences and the bondage that can come from listening to the enemy's lies.

Freedom from Addiction

There's a difference between changing a habit and breaking an addiction.

Oftentimes, people sin because they want the freedom to do what they want, regardless of whether it's right or wrong. However, one of the consequences of repeated sin is that it can rob you of that freedom. That's what happens with addiction: your mind and body become hardwired to behave in a certain way. You may decide you no longer want to use that drug or lust after those images or gamble away your paycheck, only to discover you no longer have the ability to say no. You've become an addict. You hate yourself for doing it, you know it's ruining your life, and yet you still can't stop.

There is hope for you, but you're going to need some help—more help than I can provide in this book. You've already proven, over and over, that you can't change on your own. You're not alone; many millions of people are in the same situation. There's no shame in getting help. But where can help be found?

As I've mentioned, my friend John helps run the re:generation recovery ministry at my church, and there are re:generation groups at a number of churches around the country. Celebrate Recovery is a very similar ministry and is far more common; odds are, you can find a Celebrate Recovery group somewhere in your city. I highly recommend either of them. If you don't know where to start, start there. Google them and see what's available in your area.

The important thing is that you go. Don't try to white-knuckle this on your own, thinking that this time is going to be different than the last 1,792 times that you've failed. Don't go at it alone. Invite your small group in to fight with you. Remember chapter 6? Get help. Find freedom.

It won't be an overnight change. It's probably taken you years to get to this point, so don't expect an immediate fix. Going through the twelve steps usually takes a year or more, so be prepared for that. But it's worth it. It's a matter of life and death: death from sin or true life through Christ.

> The thief comes only to steal and kill and destroy; I [Jesus] have come that they may have life, and have it to the full. (John 10:10)

Choose to live life to the fullest. You'll never regret it.

Reflection·

- What are some unhealthy patterns in your life?
- Who will you confess these to this week, and when?
- What action will you take to remove your access to temptations?
- Please take some time right now to pray for courage to pursue victory in these areas of addiction.

Adulting Forever

11
Eternity

LIFE IN PERSPECTIVE

When I was younger, the idea of "forever" would haunt me.

At that time, I didn't know where I would spend eternity. But even though I was just a kid, I did understand that eternity was a real thing, and that I would spend it *somewhere*—maybe heaven, maybe hell, or maybe just six feet underground. In a way, they all seemed scary, because of the vast amount of time I would spend there. Think about it: when you're young, even waiting until Christmas feels like "forever," and something like a century seems unfathomably long. But forever isn't measured in centuries.

In church, we'd sing "Amazing Grace," and the final verse goes like this:

> When we've been there ten thousand years,
> Bright shining as the sun,

We've no less days to sing God's praise
Than when we'd first begun.[1]

The thing about this verse is that it's actually correct. Ten thousand years into eternity, you will not be a single day closer to the end of forever. You won't be 1 percent of the way there, or 0.01 percent, or even 0.000001 percent. You will still have an eternity to go. Even after a billion years, you'll still have eternity in front of you. It *never ends*.

So I knew that I would either cease to exist and be nothing forever or go to hell and be tormented forever or go to heaven, and—I don't know—maybe sit on a cloud and play a harp forever. I didn't have a good understanding of what any of those would be like, and the sheer thought of spending forever in any of them seemed terrifying. The word *forever*, when I thought about it, sounded like the ominous quote from the movie *The Sandlot*: "For-ev-er. For-ev-er. FOR-EV-ER."

We often fear what we don't know much about. Since that time, I've learned a lot more about God and his nature, and I'm confident where I'll spend the rest of my life after earth. I know it won't be a cartoonish harp-playing festival. I believe that I will be with God in his kingdom, which is perfect and without sadness, disease, sin, or death. While that's still difficult to imagine, it doesn't stop me from trying. I think about heaven all the time. It sounds awesome, and I'm pretty excited about going there.

Though forever is now exciting, rather than scary, it is still forever. Regardless of how much longer I live in this life, whether it's one more day or seventy more years, it barely even registers as a speck compared to eternity. Sometimes when I talk to people about heaven they say, "I'm looking forward to it, but there are things I want to accomplish here first"—things like getting married or raising a family or visiting Paris or becoming successful and leaving a legacy. I can understand why they feel that way, but to be honest, that's stupid.

What is most important to you in this life is always changing. Think back to Christmastime when you were a little kid. Do you remember the anticipation of getting that one particular toy you desperately wanted? Remember how it meant *everything* to you? What was that toy for you? For me it was a scooter one year and remote-controlled car the next. Yet now, not only do we not play with those toys but also we most likely don't even have them anymore, and might struggle to even remember what they were. You can't remember the thing that once kept you up at night with anticipation. Even by high school, you would probably have laughed at the idea that the toy was important at all.

No, by high school, you had much more important things to strive toward. Do you remember what they were? Getting a letter jacket, wearing a homecoming mum or garter, getting the attention of your crush, and going to that all-important, life-defining prom. This stuff, you thought, was truly important, not that silly childhood toy. You had new things to think about at night.

Of course, once you make it to college, you're no longer sporting that letter jacket. It turns out your high school accomplishments weren't that important after all. Now, you realized what was really important: choosing a major, getting into the right fraternity or sorority, and getting a degree that will set the course of your life.

Except then you entered the real world and found out all that college stuff wasn't so important, either. There were new more important things, like getting a job, finding a place to live, and convincing someone to spend the rest of their life with you . . . it goes on and on. Don't you feel like what is important to you right now is what is really important in life? That's what you've always thought. Think about it: we always feel "now I know what is really important." Heaven will be the final realization of what actually matters, and it's not any of those things. We'll find that all those things we didn't want to miss out on in life don't really matter in an eternity where we lack nothing.

I can't wait to get there! More than once, in these conversations about heaven, I've been asked, "But don't you want to watch your kids grow up and walk your girls down the aisle at their weddings?" Yes. I certainly look forward to that day, but in no way can I compare that to the glory of heaven! I could either attend a wedding I paid for (not looking forward to that aspect of it) or attend the wedding feast of the bridegroom Jesus Christ, who invented marriage and owns the cattle on a thousand hills?! There's no decision to be made. Give me Jesus. Fortunately I don't have to decide. I woke up this morning; God trusted me with life here for another day. So my life will be lived for him.

Paul says it like this: "For me, to live is Christ and to die is gain" (Phil. 1:21). Or, as he says a couple of verses later, it is "better by far" to "depart and be with Christ" (v. 23). He knew that any day in heaven is better than any day spent on earth, and so the end of this life was actually something to look forward to. But God still had work for Paul to do on earth, and people for him to minister to (vv.

24–26), so Paul would keep working until God decided to call him home.

That's the same position we find ourselves in today. We have work to do here on earth, but it's all just a prologue before God calls us home.

The Most Important Thing

Though there is work for us to do, our performance in this life does *not* determine whether we get into heaven. That's a really important distinction.

Full disclosure: I had an editor read through a draft of this book, and she suggested that this section might not be necessary because most readers probably grew up going to church and would already know it. However, I also grew up going to church and didn't understand it at all until much later, when I was an adult. And I've talked with many people who have stories similar to mine. So I ask you, even if you think you're a Christian and you have been all your life, not to skip or gloss over what I'm about to say. It's literally the most important point in this book.

I was raised in a religious family. I went to a religious school and attended Catholic Mass twice a week, on Friday and Sunday. Get this! I literally won the "Religion Award" (yes, that's a real thing) eight of the nine years at my Catholic school. Now, I'm not bragging; this did not help me to understand who God is. To me, Christianity was defined by performing certain rituals, following a list of rules, and generally being a good person.

The main problem with this "just be good" mentality was that, despite the awards, I just wasn't that good. I was educated enough on the rules to know that I still broke them regularly. It's not like I could help it: Jesus himself said that even thinking about doing some sins still counted as being sinful itself (Matt. 5:21–28). Not that I only thought about them; I also regularly acted on those thoughts, especially as I grew older and started to enter adulthood. Eventually, I gave up any pretense of even trying. Odds are, whatever rules you've ever broken, I've probably broken them too. Sex, pornography, alcohol, drugs, materialism, an arrest record—all the usual suspects. It's the all-too-common story of someone who grew up in a Christian home and then wandered away from that lifestyle as a teenager and young adult.

So, essentially, I tried the religion thing, and then tried the you-only-live-once-so-live-for-your-own-pleasure-and-happiness thing. Both of them failed in that neither of them actually made me happy.

More importantly, I knew that neither of them would make God happy. I learned to think of God as this kind of sheriff in the sky who was looking to catch me in some wrong act. Have you ever thought about God that way? Like he's just waiting for you to mess up? I didn't want to have to deal with the choices I was making. The more I sought to enjoy life without God, the less I wanted to face him.

Why Did Jesus Have to Die?

There was one thing that I had never fully understood, though. Obviously, I had learned every single Easter about the story of Jesus: that he was the Son of God, lived on earth as a man, was killed on the cross on Good Friday, and came back to life on Easter Sunday. This is a ridiculous narrative, if you think about it. Why did Jesus have to die in the first place?

I remember asking that exact question as a kid, but I didn't get a good answer at the time (or at least I didn't understand it then). Follow me here: Jesus never did anything wrong. Unlike every other person who has ever lived, Jesus never sinned. He didn't masturbate, look at porn, get drunk, get high, or pursue many of the vices I have. He wasn't jealous, greedy, lustful, or prideful. He was perfect. This means that, out of all the people who have ever lived, Jesus least deserved to be punished in any way, let alone be given the death penalty. But that's what happened, even after multiple trials failed to find any reason to convict him (John 18:38–19:6).

Jesus is God, and God is fully in control. He proved that he was in control through miracles such as stopping a storm, walking on water, and bringing the dead back to life. Since he had control of everything from the laws of physics to death itself, that means Jesus's own death wasn't an accident or some unfortunate mistake of the justice system. He had the power to stop it. Even an average lawyer would have had the power to stop it. The crucifixion wasn't a surprise to God; it was all part of the plan. But what was the point of the plan?

Think of it this way: If what God wants from us is to just "be good," then why would Jesus have to die a slow, tortuous, publicly humiliating death for that? Couldn't Jesus just tell us to be good, show us what being good looked like, and then go on his way? I mean, dying doesn't seem to help with that plan. It kind of hurts the argument: Jesus actually was good, never made a mistake, and was killed for it anyway. That wouldn't seem to bode too well for us who try, but then fail, to live up to God's standards. People like me. People like, well, everyone. If you think you just have to be good to get to heaven, then you believe God wasted the death of his Son.

It wasn't until I was a twentysomething adult, sitting in church, still hurting from the decisions I'd made the night before, that I once again heard the gospel and understood why it was called "good news."

What's Good about Friday

See, the message Jesus brought wasn't "be good" or "follow the rules." In fact, he clarified that there was no possible way to be "good enough." Jesus spent a lot of his time explaining how even those who seemed to do everything right—the rule-following Pharisees, for instance—were far from perfect. Nobody is perfect. And yet a perfect God requires perfection from his followers.

Think about school, for an example: my sad GPA would hardly get me into a good state college, much less an Ivy League university. A lot of things in life work this way; your performance warrants your acceptance. With a place like heaven, perfection is required. Since perfection is required, no one is "good enough" to get in.

That's a problem. But God had a plan to deal with the problem.

The punishment for sin against a perfect God is not penance, prayers, good deeds, or acts of service but rather death and eternal punishment. It had been that way from the start, in Genesis 3, when animals were sacrificed to produce coverings for Adam and Eve after the first sin. It was a picture of the death produced by sin. That was especially the case with the annual Passover sacrifice—the very festival being celebrated when Jesus was killed. The sacrifices were important, because they showed that something or someone else could take on the punishment each person deserved. There had to be a payment for sin in the form of a sacrifice.

And that's why Jesus died: he was the perfect sacrifice. Since he had done nothing wrong, he wasn't due the punishment of death. But he took on that punishment in our place. Only an eternal, infinite God could take on an eternal punishment for everyone, so that's what he did. Because God is love, and there's nothing more loving you can do than willingly die to save someone else.

That's what was good about Good Friday: Jesus died in our place. He suffered the punishment we deserved. And when he came back to life, it proved he had power over death and showed what happens to all whom he saves: we may die on earth, but we are given eternal life through Jesus.

As perhaps the most famous verses in the Bible say:

> For God so loved the world that he gave his one and only Son, that whoever believes in him shall not perish but have eternal life. For God did not send his Son into the world to condemn the world, but to save the world through him. Whoever believes in him is not condemned, but whoever does not believe stands condemned already because they have not believed in the name of God's one and only Son. (John 3:16–18)

So it's not about being good enough. You can never be good enough. If you think you can be good enough, then you are trusting in yourself—not in Jesus—and that's a sin. That's the danger with religion, and that's why I would say today that I am not "religious"—I'm a hopeless sinner who is saved from myself by the miracle of Easter.

We have to stop trying to be "good enough" on our own, admit that we aren't good enough, and accept his death as payment for our sins and his resurrection as evidence that we can live forever with God. Then, the same Spirit who brought Christ back to life will come and live within us, helping us navigate life as we know it, until we are with God forever.

That's the good news that changed my life and took me from being scared and uncertain to joyful and confident. It allows me to focus on what is truly important and stop chasing after the things that, in the end, always just bring me pain. It's the most important thing for you to understand, and the most important question anyone can answer: What do you do with Jesus? Jesus, through his life, death, and resurrection, changes everything.

If this good news is old news to you, great; go and tell others. But if you haven't considered it before, or if you've heard it but, like me, didn't fully understand it, make sure you're clear on it now. Study the Bible, discuss it with your community, set up a meeting with your pastor—whatever it takes until you can be clear and confident on where you will spend eternity.

Embracing Your Real Identity

When you do trust in Christ, you become a new creation (2 Cor. 5:17). In other words, you are no longer defined by what you've done in the past. God is not judging you for your mistakes; he's forgiven and forgotten them (Ps. 103:12).

But how are you defining yourself? Where do you find your identity?

As you now know, in college, and before I was a Christian, I was a partier. And when I and my friends in Waco *really* wanted to party, we'd make the hundred-mile drive to Dallas. On one such weekend, we all decided to go to a club in Deep Ellum, which was then a clubbing district of Dallas. We made the drive with one problem in mind: while everyone else was older than twenty-one, I was still underage. I had a plan, though. My roommate would give me his ID to get in and then I'd pass it back to him. We figured that nobody really looks at the ID anyway, so they wouldn't notice that I wasn't the guy in the photo or that the bouncer was seeing the same ID twice. I would go in first, my roommate would go in last, and our other friends would go between us and pass his ID back. I know what you're thinking: I'm a genius. That's what I thought too.

When I get to the bouncer, he looks at me, looks at the ID, and starts shaking his head. "It says here that you're five-foot-nine." But I tried to play it cool. "That's a typo," I replied. "I'm five-nineteen." (If you do the math, that actually works out to six-foot-seven. Like I said, genius.)

He looks back down at the ID, still shaking his head, and reads the name out loud. "Babak Ali Hadid?" You see, my roommate was born in Iran and then moved to the United States. I, on the other hand, was not born in Iran, and I don't really look very Iranian, because I'm not.

Obviously, I hadn't thought the whole thing through very well, and my "genius" plan didn't work. It was dumb, and kind of sad, for me to pretend to be someone I was not. Yet many of us subscribe to some kind of fake identity in the way we see ourselves and define who we are.

For example, imagine if I asked you a very basic question: "Who are you?" You might answer by telling me your name. That's great, but that's just the words your parents decided to call you when you were born. It doesn't really say anything about who you are. It's more of a sound that was assigned to you. Who are you, really?

If you're in school, you might say that you're a student. But what happens when you graduate? You'll still be the same person, but you'll no longer be a student. Being a student is temporary. It's not really who you are, and it shouldn't define you as a person. Similarly, defining yourself by your job, or saying that you're a salesperson/nurse/janitor/insert career here, only describes what you currently do for about forty hours a week (which is less than a quarter of the 168 hours you get to live every week). It's still not who you are.

There are other ways you might define your identity. You might define yourself by your worldly accomplishments: your income level, your MBA degree, your state championship. You might find your identity in your earthly desires: "I love shopping," "I'm a foodie," "I can out-drink anyone." Some people get hung up on what they've done in the past: being an ex-con, getting a divorce, having an abortion. But none of those things determine who you really are.

Who you are is not your temporary role, or what you've done, or what you like to do. Who you really are, and the only identity that matters in the long run, is who you will be forever. That's an enormous statement. Think about it. The only things about you that truly count are the things that will last forever.

If you've trusted in Christ, that doesn't include the mistakes of your past; he's forgiven and removed them. It doesn't include your earthly accomplishments, because they (and the earth itself) will not last. They won't exist in eternity. And it definitely shouldn't be your earthly desires: if you find your identity in the things Christ died for, then you're not really following Christ. As the apostle Paul says in Philippians 3:18–19, people who identify with and embrace their sinful appetites "live as enemies of the cross of Christ."

In fact, much of Philippians 3 talks about where we should (or shouldn't) find our identity. In it, Paul lays out all of the things he could find identity in. He was religious, zealous, well-educated, born into the right family in the right country, and faultless when it came to following the law. Yet he said he considered all those things "garbage" compared to his identity as a follower of Christ.

Before Paul became a Christian, he was the number-one enemy of Christians, going to great lengths to ensure they were either jailed or killed. So, if anyone could be condemned by God for things they'd done in the past, then surely he would have been. Yet he became, after that, the greatest missionary and proponent of Christianity the world has ever seen, showing us that no sin disqualifies us from being used by God.

Instead of finding his identity in his past, his accomplishments, or his earthly desires, Paul focused on who he would be eternally. "Their mind is set on earthly things," he said. "But our citizenship is in heaven" (vv. 19–20). Paul was a Roman citizen, which was the most valuable and sought-after ID you could have at that time. But he considered himself first and foremost a citizen of heaven who only had a temporary visa here on earth.

If heaven required an ID card to get in the door, that ID wouldn't list any of your earthly accomplishments, failures, memberships, or affiliations. It wouldn't matter where you were born, what school you went to, how much money you made over the course of your career, whether you had a criminal record, or whether you got that date to prom. The only ID God would be checking is your identity in Christ. The only good work that can get you in is the work that Christ accomplished on the cross.

So, as you live out this relatively short life, focus on your true identity. Remind yourself of it daily. Don't discount your worth or hold yourself back because of a past that no longer defines you or mistakes that have been fully forgiven and won't mark you in eternity. Don't focus on temporary, worldly accomplishments that will also be forgotten. Live as who you are: a citizen of heaven, an adopted son or daughter of the King of all creation, temporarily on an earthly assignment until your Father calls you home.

Live for the Longer

One goal of this book is to help things go well with you in this life. As a young adult, you potentially have several decades of earthly life left to go, which can seem like a really long time.

But remember, forever is a really, really, *really* long time.

Compared to eternity, your life here on earth is less than a speck. Less than one grain of sand compared to all the beaches in all the world. Your life is a tiny dot on an eternal timeline.

Do you know anything about your great-great-grandfather? Do you know his name? Do you know what he did for a living? Do you know where he lived? Do you know what his favorite color was, or how old he was when he was married?

Most likely this man was alive about fifty years ago. He is part of your family; without him, you never would have been born. Yet you probably know very little about him. What this means is that fifty years after you've died, no one will be enamored by the way you lived this life—not even your own great-great-grandchild.

Sure, how you live matters to you right now, and it matters to your family and the people around you. But any earthly accomplishments won't really seem like that big of a deal a billion years from now. What matters in eternity are the things that will last for eternity.

There's an old saying I sometimes hear people quote: "Don't be so heavenly minded that you're no earthly good." The idea behind the expression is that if you're focused on the reality of eternity, you'll somehow waste your time here on earth. After all, this life is so short, and eternity is what really matters.

It might sound catchy and convincing, but it's simply not true. In fact, we're specifically told by God to be heavenly minded; in Colossians 3:2, it says to "Set your minds on things above, not on earthly things." And 1 John 2:15 says, "Do not love the world or anything in the world. If anyone loves the world, love for the Father is not in them."

The truth is, being "heavenly minded" is the one way to ensure you don't waste your time on earth. It means that you will be focused on things that truly last. And what here on earth will truly last? People. The finest house, the grandest monument, the greatest collection of earthly treasures: these will all one day, much sooner than you think, be gone and forgotten. But every person you see, from the best-dressed billionaire to the homeless woman wearing rags, is an eternal creature.

They will last forever, somewhere. If you do something that helps somebody, that action will be remembered forever. Most importantly, if you help point someone to the truth of eternity, that person can then join you in heaven forever.

Besides, being "heavenly minded" actually provides a much bigger incentive to be "earthly good." It's basic economics. Many people work hard to save up money for retirement or to build homes here on earth that are bigger and nicer. They study and search and pay experts to figure out which investments will provide the best return over time, so they get the most out of their income from work. They calculate return on investment (ROI) and net present value (NPV), all while accounting for the risk that whatever money they invest they might end up losing instead.

But if you live with the knowledge that you'll be in heaven forever, the investment calculations change. Because God makes it very clear that he will reward us in heaven for the good things we do here on earth. We're not talking about earning salvation as a reward; eternal life itself is a free gift. But within that eternal life there are rewards. For example, in Matthew 19:21, Jesus tells a rich man that if he gives his earthly possessions to the poor, he "will have treasure in heaven." First Corinthians 3 shows that those who share the gospel and disciple other believers will be rewarded for their work. In Matthew 10:41–42, Jesus says that even the smallest deed (giving another believer a cup of water) can earn a reward. And in Matthew 6:19–21, he tells us:

> Do not store up for yourselves treasures on earth, where moths and vermin destroy, and where thieves break in and steal. But store up for yourselves treasures in heaven, where

moths and vermin do not destroy, and where thieves do not break in and steal.

Before proposing to my wife, I remember shopping for an engagement ring and being blown away by how much they cost. I quickly learned that it's not the gold band that makes them so expensive (even though the gold is plenty expensive enough). Most of the cost came from the price of the diamond. At one time, diamonds actually weren't that popular; sales were on the decline, and if you know anything about supply and demand, a lack of demand leads to a lower price. But then De Beers, which controls much of the world's diamond supply, came up with the advertising slogan, "A diamond is forever." Sales took off. The campaign was so successful that nearly everyone today has heard of the phrase, and *Advertising Age* ranked it as the best advertising slogan of the century.[2] Often we ascribe value to something based on how enduring it is, and since diamonds supposedly last forever, we automatically assume they must be the most valuable material.

It's a good slogan, but technically diamonds do not last forever. Sure, as the hardest natural substance on earth, they'll last longer than most anything else you could buy. But no material thing on earth truly lasts forever. On earth, things wear out, break down, get old, lose value, or get stolen. Eventually, everything on earth will turn to dust or otherwise be destroyed. In heaven, though, everything does last forever. And that makes a huge difference when you're trying to decide what to invest in. Something that lasts forever and provides you with benefits for all eternity is far more valuable than something that will last only a few years or only a lifetime. In fact, an eternal treasure is *infinitely* more valuable than a temporary earthly treasure. The ROI is infinity. It is literally the best investment you could ever make. Our problem is that we struggle to believe this.

If we believe that our good works and generosity here on earth provide an infinite return on investment, we should be motivated to invest even more. Instead of being "no earthly good," believers in Christ should do the most good. It's what Christians have been known for throughout most of history: selflessly loving and serving others, even when it doesn't seem to make sense from an earthly perspective. We build homes for others instead of building bigger ones for ourselves because we know we have an eternal home being built for us. We take care of the sick and dying, even though it puts us at risk of catching the disease ourselves, because we know we'll have eternal life no matter what. (See also the black plague, when Christians were often the only ones who would help people with the disease, and they did so joyfully, knowing that they only risked expediting their journey to paradise.) We give selflessly because we're not seeking to build up our own glory here on earth.

Diamonds do not last forever. Treasures stored in heaven do. If you buy a stock on the stock market, it might increase in value, but it might not—and, regardless, it will be worthless to you in eighty years (because you're dead). Or you can buy stock that appreciates in value and yields dividends in eternity. Invest in that stock!

Don't Wait

When I became a pastor, one of my first responsibilities was to help with a funeral. A very wealthy man had died and had left his wealth to his two sons. Since his sons were in their twenties, and I was the young adult pastor, I was asked to go with our senior pastor to visit the family.

We drove into the wealthy part of Dallas, with big houses on huge plots of land. We turned onto a cobblestone drive and followed it to a big wooden gate by a guard house. The gate opened slowly and revealed a whole estate behind it: a meticulously manicured lawn; landscaped gardens bursting with pink, red, and purple flowers; and an enormous white house. We parked and went inside the house. Everything was huge. The hallways were big. The furniture was big. The paintings were big. I had never seen anything like it! We sat down with the two grieving sons and asked them about their father so that we could prepare for doing his funeral.

Although the house was near perfect in its presentation, I noticed that there were little yellow sticky notes all over the walls. They didn't seem to belong in such a well-kept place. "What are those notes?" I asked. "In his last days," the sons explained, "Dad wanted to be surrounded with the Word of God. So he had us write Bible verses out and put them all over the house." Their father had not always been a Christian, but when he had been faced with his mortality through a life-threatening disease, he had become one.

Curious, I asked them to tell me more about what their dad had done in his last days. "Well, he would share the gospel with anyone and everyone," they said. "He'd call in the doctors and nurses to tell them about Jesus. He'd have us bring in people for him to share with." Death can be a motivator in that way. You begin to see your priorities differently.

"What else did he do?" I asked. I wanted to hear more how this man, who was so successful by the world's standards, had prioritized his last days on earth. "He tried to give away all of his money. He wanted to know about charities in need. He wanted to resource the church with his wealth. He was frustrated when he couldn't. It was locked up in trusts, and moving it required attorneys, brokers, and meetings." Their father had gone to great lengths to secure his money and save it up for the future—a future he later found out would be cut off much earlier than he had planned. Now that money belonged to his two sons. It was their money—or at least it was theirs to steward, like it had been their dad's to steward.

I asked if there was anything else they'd like to share about their dad. The two sons looked at each other and said in unison, "He said: 'Don't wait.'" They explained that, as death crept up on their father, he would cry out, "Don't wait! Don't wait, like I did! Go and tell them about Jesus! Live for Jesus!"

Today, I pass that advice on to you. Don't wait. Don't live most of your life focused on temporary things, thinking you'll have time later on to think about eternity. Focus on what really matters now. Surround yourself with the truth of God. Share the love of Christ often. Give generously to those in need, and share the resources God has temporarily entrusted to you.

This life is short. The average life expectancy in the United States today is about seventy-eight years, so you can take your current age and do the math. That's the average; we never know how soon our lives may end. But we can be sure of where we'll be eternally, and live now in the light of that fact. Don't wait.

Reflection

- What do you think heaven will be like?
- How certain are you that you will get there?
- If God asked you, "Why should I let you in?" what would you say?
- How can you commit to living the rest of your life on earth for eternity?
- If you literally believed that you were going to die and be with God forever, what changes would you make?

Acknowledgments

Special thanks to:

Monica Pokluda: you are by far the single most loving person I've ever met. And I get to be married to you #grace. Adulting is easier, and way more fun, with you.

Presley, Finley, and Weston: you all are a bank full of sermon illustrations. Thank you for letting me share your stories. I've learned so much about God's love through loving you.

Mom and Dad: you are amazing parents; I was simply rebellious. Thank you for pouring a foundation and pointing me in the right direction.

Todd Wagner: I learned about the grace of the gospel from you. You are the best leader I've ever met, and I get to call you friend. I'm eternally grateful.

Kevin McConaghy: you have partnered with me in this project, and I'm so thankful for the ways God has gifted you and for how you steward those gifts.

David Marvin: you will lead the next generation of the church. I'm in the foxhole with you. Thank you for warring with me against evil.

Emily Corley: the trains would stop without you. Thank you for keeping them running on time.

Don Gates: you called at just the right time and have been a tremendous supporter of this book. Thank you for believing in me.

Rebekah Guzman: you gave me a chance. Thank you for caring about the future of the church.

My community group: you are the best examples of Christ-followers I know. Thank you for always pointing me to him.

My colaborers in the gospel: I work with the most gifted people I know. Thank you for being awesome. You are a team and a family.

The Porch: thank you for chasing Jesus and trading in the American dream for more of him. You will never regret it.

Notes

Chapter 1 Life

1. My colaborer Jeff Parker.

2. Matt McCreary, "Depression and Work: The Impact of Depression on Different Generations of Employees," *Morneau Shepell*, accessed October 20, 2017, https://www.bensingerdupont.com/filebin/pdfpublic /Whitepaper_MorneauShepell_Depression_and_work_E-US_0417.pdf; Jesse Signal, "For 80 Years, Young Americans Have Been Getting More Anxious and Depressed, and No One Is Quite Sure Why," *The Cut*, March 13, 2016, https://www.thecut.com/2016/03/for-80-years-young-americans -have-been-getting-more-anxious-and-depressed.html.

Chapter 2 Purpose

1. S.H.A.P.E. was originally used by Rick Warren, *The Purpose Driven Life* (Grand Rapids: Zondervan, 2002).

Chapter 3 Authority

1. "Public Trust in Government: 1958–2017," *Pew Research Center*, May 3, 2017, http://www.people-press.org/2017/05/03/public-trust-in -government-1958-2017/.

2. Suetonius, *Life of Nero*; Tacitus, *Histories* and *Annals*; Cassius Dio, *Roman History*.

3. Also the *Code of Hammurabi*, Law #117.

4. See M. L. Bush, *Serfdom and Slavery: Studies in Legal Bondage* (Abingdon, UK: Routledge, 1996).

5. See Kwame Anthony Appiah and Martin Bunzl, *Buying Freedom: The Ethics and Economics of Slave Redemption* (Princeton, NJ: Princeton University Press, 2007).

6. Michael Marlowe, "Make Good Use of Your Servitude: Some Observations on Biblical Interpretation and Slavery," *Bible Research*, October 2003, http://www.bible-researcher.com/slavery.html.

7. Erica Anderson, "Why You're Having a Hard Time with Your Millennial Employees—and What to Do about It," *Forbes*, May 9, 2016, https://www.forbes.com/sites/erikaandersen/2016/05/09/why-youre-having-a-hard-time-with-your-millennial-employees-and-what-to-do-about-it/#63bef61041c5.

8. Joel Stein, "Millennials: The Me Me Me Generation," *Time*, May 20, 2013, http://time.com/247/millennials-the-me-me-me-generation/; Sean Bisceglia, "Outside Opinion: Millennials Frustrate HR Execs," *Chicago Tribune*, September 5, 2014, http://www.chicagotribune.com/business/ct-hiring-millennials-outside-opinion-0907-biz-20140905-story.html.

9. "Job Seeker Nation Study 2016," *Jobvite*, accessed October 20 2017, https://www.jobvite.com/wp-content/uploads/2016/03/Jobvite_Jobseeker_Nation_2016.pdf; Val Matta, "Why 60% of Millennial Workers Are Quitting," *Business Insider*, December 30, 2013, http://www.businessinsider.com/why-60-percent-of-your-millennial-workers-are-quitting-2013-12.

10. Michael Lipka and Claire Gecewicz, "More Americans Now Say They're Spiritual but Not Religious," *Pew Research Center*, September 6, 2017, http://www.pewresearch.org/fact-tank/2017/09/06/more-americans-now-say-theyre-spiritual-but-not-religious/.

Chapter 4 Work

1. See Thom S. Rainer, *The Millennials: Connecting to America's Largest Generation* (Nashville: B&H Publishing Group, 2011).

Chapter 5 Money

1. First Kings 10:14 says that Solomon received 666 talents of gold annually. Since a talent weighed about 75 pounds, that equals 49,950 pounds, or about 25 tons. In 2017, gold was worth an average of about $1,250 per troy ounce, which makes Solomon's income over $910 million, "not including the revenues from merchants and traders and from all the Arabian kings and the governors of the territories" (1 Kings 10:15).

2. Daniel Kahneman and Angus Deaton, "High Income Improves Evaluation of Life but Not Emotional Well-Being," *Proceedings of the National Academy of Sciences of the United States of America*, August 4, 2010, http://www.pnas.org/content/107/38/16489.full.

3. Andrew Meldrum, "Where a Basketful of Groceries Costs a Bucketful of Cash," *The Guardian*, August 17, 2006, https://www.theguardian.com/business/2006/aug/17/Zimbabwenews.internationalnews.

4. Paulina Pchelin and Ryan T. Howell, "The Hidden Cost of Value-Seeking: People Do Not Accurately Forecast the Economic Benefits of Experiential Purchases," *The Journal of Positive Psychology*, March 31, 2014, http://www.tandfonline.com/doi/abs/10.1080/17439760.2014.898316; Amit Kumar et al., "Waiting for Merlot: Anticipatory Consumption of Experiential and Material Purchases," *Association for Psychological Science*, August 21, 2014, *Sage Journals*, http://journals.sagepub.com/doi/abs/10.1177/0956797614546556.

5. E. W. Dunn et al., "Spending Money on Others Promotes Happiness," *Science*, May 29, 2009, https://www.ncbi.nlm.nih.gov/pubmed/18356530.

Chapter 6 Community

1. Miller McPherson et al., "Social Isolation in America: Changes in Core Discussion Networks over Two Decades," *American Sociological Review*, June 2006, http://journals.sagepub.com/doi/abs/10.1177/000312240607100301.

2. Jo Griffin, "The Lonely Society," *The Mental Health Foundation*, 2010, https://www.mentalhealth.org.uk/sites/default/files/the_lonely society_report.pdf; M. Luhmann and L. C. Hawkley, "Age Differences in Loneliness from Late Adolescence to Oldest Old Age," *Developmental Psychology*, June 2016, https://www.ncbi.nlm.nih.gov/pubmed/27148782.

3. "2011 Relationships Indicators Survey," *Relationships Australia*, 2011, http://www.rasa.org.au/media-centre/relationships-indicator-survey-2011/#.

4. Aaron Smith, "6 New Facts about Facebook," *Pew Research Center*, February 3, 2014, http://www.pewresearch.org/fact-tank/2014/02/03/6-new-facts-about-facebook/.

Chapter 7 Conflict

1. Drake Baer, "America's Top Couples Therapist Says All Successful Marriages Share This Trait," *Business Insider*, January 28, 2015, http://www.businessinsider.com/successful-marriages-share-this-trait-2015-1.

2. The WENI acronym is from the team at Watermark Community Church in Dallas, and it's based on the work of Scott Stanley and his colleagues. See also Scott Stanley, Daniel Trathen, Savanna McCain, and B. Milton Bryan, *A Lasting Promise: A Christian Guide to Fighting for Your Marriage*, second ed. (San Francisco: Jossey-Bass, 2014).

Chapter 8 Dating

1. Wendy Wang and Kim Parker, "Record Share of Americans Have Never Married," *Pew Research Center*, September 24, 2014, http://www.pewsocialtrends.org/2014/09/24/record-share-of-americans-have-never-married/.

2. "Historical Marital Status Tables," *United States Census Bureau*, November 2017, https://www.census.gov/data/tables/time-series/demo/families/marital.html.

3. Alexander A. Plateris, "100 Years of Marriage and Divorce Statistics: 1867–1967," *U.S. Department of Health, Education, and Welfare*, December 1973, https://www.cdc.gov/nchs/data/series/sr_21/sr21_024.pdf.

4. "Statistical Abstract of the United States: 2012," *United States Census Bureau*, August 2011, https://www.census.gov/library/publications/2011/compendia/statab/131ed.html.

5. See Moira Wiegel, *Labor of Love: The Invention of Dating* (New York: Farrar, Straus and Giroux, 2016).

6. To quote Wikipedia: "Historically, premarital sex was considered a moral issue which was taboo in many cultures and considered a sin by a number of religions, but since about the 1960s, it has become more widely accepted, especially in Western countries" ("Premarital Sex," Wikipedia, accessed January 16, 2018, https://en.wikipedia.org/wiki/Premarital_sex).

7. Tara C. Jatlaoui et al., "Abortion Surveillance—United States, 2013," *Centers for Disease Control and Prevention*, November 25, 2016, https://www.cdc.gov/mmwr/volumes/65/ss/ss6512a1.htm.

8. Thanks to the invention of new types of contraceptives, there are now more birth control options than ever before, and many of them are free with insurance (or are handed out freely at clinics and schools).

9. R. K. Jones et al., "More Than Poverty: Disruptive Events among Women Having Abortions in the USA," *Journal of Family Planning and Reproductive Health Care*, 2013, https://www.ncbi.nlm.nih.gov/pubmed/22906858.

10. "Historical Marital Status Tables," *United States Census Bureau*.

11. "Historical Marital Status Tables," *United States Census Bureau*.

12. Nicholas H. Wolfinger, "Counterintuitive Trends in the Link between Premarital Sex and Marital Stability," *Institute for Family Studies*, June 6, 2016, https://ifstudies.org/blog/counterintuitive-trends-in-the-link-between-premarital-sex-and-marital-stability/.

13. Jeremy Wiles, "Science Proves Premarital Sex Rewires the Brain," *Charisma News*, May 11, 2013, https://www.charismanews.com/opinion/39405-science-proves-premarital-sex-rewires-the-brain.

14. Wiles, "Science Proves Premarital Sex Rewires the Brain"; Taryn Hillin, "New Study Claims People Who've Had More Sexual Partners Report Unhappier Marriages," *The Huffington Post*, August 22, 2014, https://www.huffingtonpost.com/2014/08/21/more-sexual-partners-un happy-marriage_n_5698440.html.

15. See, for example, Scott M. Stanley et al., "Sliding Versus Deciding: Inertia and the Premarital Cohabitation Effect," *Family Relations*, September 7, 2006, https://www.ncbi.nlm.nih.gov/pmc/articles/PMC3656416/; Catherine L. Cohan and Stacey Kleinbaum, "Toward a Greater Understanding of the Cohabitation Effect: Premarital Cohabitation and Marital Communication," *Journal of Marriage and Family*, February 2002, http:// onlinelibrary.wiley.com/doi/10.1111/j.1741-3737.2002.00180.x/abstract; David R. Hall and John Z. Zhao, "Cohabitation and Divorce in Canada: Testing the Selectivity Hypothesis," *Journal of Marriage and Family*, May 1995, https://www.questia.com/library/journal/1P3-6663599/co habitation-and-divorce-in-canada-testing-the-selectivity. There are many such studies.

16. Arielle Kuperberg, "Age at Coresidence, Premarital Cohabitation, and Marriage Dissolution: 1985–2009," *Journal of Marriage and Family*, March 4, 2014, http://onlinelibrary.wiley.com/doi/10.1111/jomf.12092 /abstract.

17. Linda J. Waite et al., "Does Divorce Make People Happy? Findings from a Study of Unhappy Marriages," *Institute for American Values*, 2002, http://americanvalues.org/catalog/pdfs/does_divorce_make_people _happy.pdf.

Chapter 9 Worry

1. Ronald C. Kessler et al., "The Global Burden of Mental Disorders: An Update from the WHO World Mental Health (WMH) Surveys," *Epidemiologia e Psichiatria Sociale*, Jan–Mar 2009, 18(1): 23–33, https:// www.ncbi.nlm.nih.gov/pubmed/19378696.

2. Norman B. Anderson et al., "Stress in America: Paying with Our Health," *American Psychological Association*, February 4, 2015, https:// www.apa.org/news/press/releases/stress/2014/stress-report.pdf.

3. T. M. Luhrmann, "The Anxious Americans," *New York Times*, July 18, 2015, https://www.nytimes.com/2015/07/19/opinion/sunday/the -anxious-americans.html.

4. Tom C. Russ et al., "Association between Psychological Distress and Mortality: Individual Participant Pooled Analysis of 10 Prospective Cohort Studies," *BMJ*, 2012, http://www.bmj.com/content/345/bmj.e4933.

5. Twitter post, @timkellernyc, February 15, 2015, https://twitter.com /timkellernyc/status/567061295783223297?lang=en.

Chapter 10 Recovery

1. Garry Mulholland, "Amy Winehouse at the BBC Review," *BBC*, November 12, 2012, http://www.bbc.co.uk/music/reviews/zv28/.

2. Paul Bentley, "A Death Foretold: The Rapid Rise and Tragic Fall of Amy Winehouse, the Deeply Flawed Soul Prodigy," *Daily Mail*, July 25, 2011, http://www.dailymail.co.uk/tvshowbiz/article-2018025/Amy-Wine house-dead-Before-rise-fall-deeply-flawed-prodigy.html.

Chapter 11 Eternity

1. "Amazing Grace," John Newton (1779).

2. "Ad Age Advertising Century: Top 10 Slogans," *Ad Age*, March 29, 1999, http://adage.com/article/special-report-the-advertising-century/ad -age-advertising-century-top-10-slogans/140156/.

About the Author

Jonathan "JP" Pokluda is the Dallas campus pastor of Watermark Community Church in the Dallas-Fort Worth area. Under his leadership, The Porch, Watermark's ministry for young adults, has grown to become one of the largest gatherings of twenty- and thirtysomethings in the world. The Porch reaches over four thousand young adults who attend weekly gatherings in the Dallas-Fort Worth area and tens of thousands more who listen to The Porch all across the United States.

After growing up in several different church denominations, JP came to understand the grace of the gospel in his early twenties. This ignited a desire in him to inspire young adults to radically follow Jesus Christ, and unleash them to change the world. JP's belief that twenty- and thirtysomethings are the most underleveraged demographic in the church inspired him to write *Welcome to Adulting: Navigating Faith, Friendship, Finances, and the Future.*

JP has taught all over the world, but the ministry he is most passionate about is his family. JP and his wife of thirteen years, Monica, live in Dallas, Texas, with their three children: Presley, Finley, and Weston.

To learn more about The Porch—or stream weekly gatherings live—visit theporch.live.

JONATHAN POKLUDA

————————— CONNECT WITH JP —————————

 Jonathan Pokluda | @JPokluda | @JPokluda

Dear world-changer,

First, I want to sincerely thank you for investing in this book. While there are many trials today, when I think about the future of the church I am very hopeful. I believe that God is preparing you for such a time as this. One of the concerns that I have for the church is our worship of people and "celebrity pastors." I want you to know that I would much rather you follow Jesus than me. With that said, I still love to connect with other Jesus followers, and I am always encouraged by hearing about what God is doing through young adults around the world. If you'd like to connect, there are some tools above that can help! I am praying for you as I write this, that you are connected to a local Bible-teaching church, and if you are ever in Dallas, please come and say "hi" at Watermark Community Church.

Adulting with you,

Jonathan Pokluda

The Porch is a gathering of thousands of young adults who meet every Tuesday night at 7PM at Watermark Community Church in Dallas, Texas. This worship service is also streamed to The Porch Live campuses around the world and online at www.theporch.live and The Porch App. Any given Tuesday we address the challenges that face twenty- and thirtysomethings with relevant biblical teaching and worship through music. We are seeking to change the world through the lives of young adults in the name and for the fame of Jesus Christ.

   | www.theporch.live

FOLLOW THE PORCH ON SOCIAL MEDIA
for the latest messages, events, and information

 the porch dallas | @theporch | @theporch